If you had put $10,000 into the equity portion of the
Rainbow Portfolio in 1973, you would have earned $920,180
by December 31, 2007. That's more than *twice as much* as the
S&P 500 index and more than *three times as much* as the
average stock fund. Turn to page 115 to learn how to start
investing in the Rainbow Portfolio today.

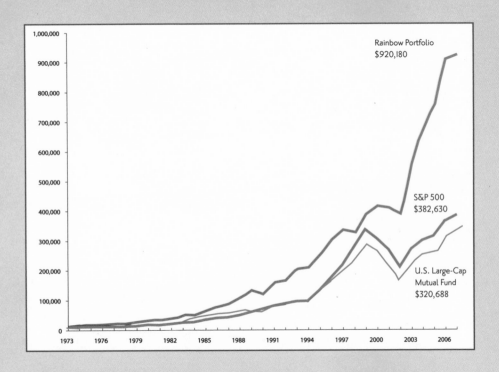

Rainbow Portfolio performance compared to S&P 500 and average
U.S. Large-Cap Mutual Fund for $10,000 invested January 1, 1973,
through December 31, 2007

THE CURE FOR
MONEY
MADNESS

THE CURE FOR
MONEY

MADNESS

Break Your Bad Money Habits,

Live Without Financial Stress—and

Make More Money!

SPENCER SHERMAN

BROADWAY BOOKS

NEW YORK

BROADWAY

Published in the United States by Broadway Books, an imprint of The Doubleday
Publishing Group, a division of Random House, Inc., New York.
www.broadwaybooks.com

BROADWAY BOOKS and its logo, a letter B bisected on the diagonal,
are trademarks of Random House, Inc.

This book is designed to provide accurate and authoritative information on the subject of
personal finances. While all of the stories and anecdotes described in the book are based on true
experiences, most of the names are pseudonyms, and some situations have been changed slightly for
educational purposes and to protect each individual's privacy. It is sold with the understanding that
neither the Author nor the Publisher is engaged in rendering legal, accounting, or other professional
services by publishing this book. As each individual situation is unique, questions relevant to personal
finances and specific to the individual should be addressed to an appropriate professional to ensure
that the situation has been evaluated carefully and appropriately. The Author and Publisher
specifically disclaim any liability, loss, or risk that is incurred as a consequence, directly
or indirectly, of the use and application of any of the contents of this work.

Book design by Diane Hobbing of Snap-Haus Graphics

Library of Congress Cataloging-in-Publication Data
Sherman, Spencer D.
The cure for money madness : break your bad money habits, live without
financial stress—and make more money! / Spencer Sherman.
p.   cm.
Includes index.
1. Finance, Personal. 2. Investments. I. Title.
HG179.S4618 2009
332.024—dc22
2008031688

ISBN 978-0-7679-2855-7

PRINTED IN THE UNITED STATES OF AMERICA

1   3   5   7   9   10   8   6   4   2

First Edition

TO MY CHILDREN,

Jeremy and Talia—

AND TO ALL CHILDREN:

may they feel joy, peace, and abundance,

regardless of how much money they have

"*The difficulty lies not so much in developing new ideas
as in escaping old ones.*"
—John M. Keynes

"*October. This is one of the peculiarly dangerous months
to speculate. The others are July, January, September,
April, November, May, March, June, December,
August, and February.*"
—Mark Twain

"*Behind the complicated details of the world stand the simplicities.*"
—Graham Greene

CONTENTS

ACKNOWLEDGMENTS

My next book, as I tell anyone who will listen, will be entitled *Everybody Should Write a Book*, for I have found authorship to be the most challenging and rewarding of experiences. But I didn't do it alone, and I want to acknowledge and thank the many people who helped me turn my ideas into a book.

I am profoundly grateful to renowned marriage therapist and international workshop leader Anne Watts. The moment that we decided to join forces and create our Financial Intimacy workshops was the beginning of our commitment to take our message to a wider audience. Throughout the process, Anne has been my mentor, my friend, my public speaking coach, and my helpmate in writing this book. There would be no *Cure for Money Madness* without Anne.

Defying the conventional wisdom about the dangers of doing business with friends was one of my most successful and rewarding acts. Brent Kessel is my dear friend and my trusted colleague and business partner. He urged me to take a risk and do what my family had consistently failed at—partner in business with someone who is (practically) family. His life, his work, his beautiful family, and his own book, *It's Not About the Money*, have been inspirations for me, and I thank him for helping me flourish in innumerable ways.

My friend Reavis Moore was one of the first people to see a book in my ideas, and he introduced me to Bob Levine, my agent *extraordinaire*. I'm still astonished that Bob can be so fierce, say "no" so often, and yet be so incredibly generous and easy to love.

It was Bob who put me together with two women who played key roles in the book: Susan Dworkin, who gave the book its incredible and, as it turns out, absolutely prescient title; and Susanna Margolis, who helped me clarify my ideas with patience and common sense.

I am pleased to acknowledge and thank my wonderful colleagues at Random House: Kris Puopolo, my editor, who helped me sift through the dirt to get to the gold, the selfless and understated David

Drake, Julie Sills, Catherine Pollock, and Stephanie Bowen. I am grateful also to my team in California for helping me to disseminate the cure far and wide: Jesse Seaver, Maria Freebairn-Smith, Savala Nolan, and Janine Sternlieb.

I was well along in the process of writing the book when I had the opportunity to meet the legendary Byron Katie. The instant rapport we shared and the seemingly automatic meshing of our work have been a profound joy to me. The Work of Byron Katie and her life-transforming Four Questions are a powerful resource for curing money madness.

So many other people—teachers, friends, family, clients, and workshop participants—have contributed to the writing of *The Cure for Money Madness*. I reach back to my earliest influences, starting with my late parents: my father, Lester, who gave me permission to speak my mind even if no one agrees with what I have to say, and my mother, Phyllis, who gave me the sense that everyone is my friend. I am immensely grateful also to my very-much-alive dear sister, Carol, for showing me the value of a sense of humor. I am grateful to the three of them for their immense love and support.

Mordecai Mitnick was instrumental in helping me understand my own money madness so I could explain the cure. Charlie Fisher and Maury Stein, Brandeis professors who became close friends and mentors, provided valuable critical feedback on the manuscript. So did Pat Jennerjohn, Marty Dirks, Jonathan Marks, Brian Kennedy, Brian Heath, Billy White, Karen Solomon, and lifelong friend Bennett Cohen.

Jason Cole, my business partner and friend, helped me to focus on what I really love doing in the financial world and thereby helped create much of the material for this book. All the employees of Abacus have helped me to think outside the box—essential both for our business and for this book. Their community of support and collegiality has brought me a great deal of joy. In particular I must acknowledge Greg Aloia and Suzanne Lawrence, who have been long-term loyal and supportive colleagues at Abacus.

Paul Jaffe, owner of one of the last remaining independent book chains, Copperfield's, was another friend who saw the book in what I was doing and encouraged me to go forward.

Jocelyn Rasmussen, friend, coach, and all-around inspiration, gave me the confidence that my ideas could actually help people. She has been a steadfast cheerleader of both my life and this book.

Lenny Linsker offered me the use of that most prized commodity, a Manhattan apartment, so I could finish the manuscript.

Many people have served as mentors for this work, whether they know it or not: David Michael; Frank Donoghue, a once-and-current writing mentor; and George Kinder, a financial advisor I respect enormously and the man who launched me into the workshop arena. Al Winner was the first mentor in my life.

In providing emotional support, friends from every corner of my life helped make this book possible and enriched the writing process. B. J. Wasserman, Michael and Donna Stusser, Chris Deckker, Geralyn Gendreau, artists Alex and Allyson Grey, Bex Wilkinson, Josh Mailman, Parker Johnson, Dana Zed, and my dear lifelong friend and college roommate, Howard Levine, all provided the kind of steadfast encouragement that is so essential to the writing process.

My men's group—Rick Phillips, Tom Sipes, Saha Johnson, Tom Wick, Jahn Ballard, Murray Lewis, and the late Andy Davidson—was also a bulwark of support on more than 400 Monday nights over ten years. The collective wisdom and loving presence of these friends helped me share my money secrets, keep my money monster at bay, cure my own money madness, and stay madness-free.

From the world of established authors, I am grateful to exercise guru Kathy Smith, to Deepak Chopra, and to QVC host Kathy Levine, who can sell anything. All provided early encouragement that gave me confidence in my ideas.

I am deeply grateful to my wife, Janine, for her enthusiasm for my ideas, for her editing skills, for being my partner in financial intimacy, and for her love. I am also grateful to the two most extraordinary beings and teachers in my life, Jeremy and Talia, who remind me daily that my net worth is so much larger than I could possibly calculate.

Finally, I want to acknowledge my first cousins, Steven Gilbert and Jane Shelofsky. Even though money madness drove our families apart for decades, our recent reunion is proof that anything, even a fight over money, can be healed.

THE UNCHALLENGED ASSUMPTIONS
OF MONEY MADNESS

Here is a set of assumptions, almost universally accepted as true, that block rational thinking about money. These unexamined beliefs can make us behave in ways that are disastrous to our bottom line and our peace of mind. *The Cure for Money Madness* will challenge these assumptions and give you the antidote to your unproductive money behavior.

Assumption	Challenge/Antidote
I don't want to know the numbers/what my bank statement says/what my taxes are/what my credit card debt is because I might get worried.	The numbers are never as scary as the assumption. *Antidote:* Check your Actual Net Worth™ to see that you are wealthier than you think (see Chapter 10).
I don't know anything about money, so I let my spouse handle it; I don't have anything valuable to say where money is concerned.	Money is simpler than you think. Your natural common sense is worth as much as if not more than your spouse's financial sophistication.
I'm a teacher/musician/civil servant and can never make more than _____.	This is limited thinking—first, because it doesn't value all the fringe benefits of your total compensation package and, second, because plenty of teachers/musicians/civil servants have come up with creative ways to make additional money.

Assumption	Challenge/Antidote
I can't live without credit cards.	Everyone lived without credit cards until about 50 years ago, and many people live just fine without them today. *Antidote:* Keep one for emergencies, and pay cash as you go.
There's a recession; I need to sell my house/stock portfolio/jewelry/ art collection.	Historically, whatever goes down eventually goes up again. *Antidote:* Recession is an opportunity to buy.
My salary is $48,000; that means I have $4,000 a month to spend.	Not true. Your after-tax salary is what you have to spend; that $4,000 per month is really about $3,000 per month. *Antidote:* Delete the pre-tax salary figure from your mind; it's a fiction.
The stock market is risky.	Buying an individual stock may be risky, but the stock market over its history has proven to be a very solid investment. Those who lose in the stock market typically have concentrated their investing to try to make a killing, rather than diversifying to achieve steady returns over periods of ten years or more.
I can't afford to save anything.	How about $1 a day? Or $5 a day? Of course, you can save something, and you should: Start exercising your saving muscle so you begin to see yourself as a saver rather than as a spender or debtor.

Assumption	Challenge/Antidote
I don't know where my money goes.	Take a look: Check out your monthly cash flow statement (see Chapter 5). And if you really want your money to "go" someplace in particular, put it there first; for example, if you want to pay off your credit card debt, make that the first check you write this month.
I was solicited so often by this charity that I finally had to give them something.	Write down your charitable intentions—and give proactively, not reactively (see Chapter 9).
I have to leave my money to my kids.	Is that really what they need? Is it really what you want? Will a legacy rob your children of some vigor in their lives? Will it send the wrong message? Consider setting up a donor-advised fund that enables them to give away the money.
Renting is throwing money down the drain.	Do you want to make the biggest spending decision of your life without considering the rental option (see Chapter 8)?
My assets are increasing, so my net worth is going up.	But your debt may be going up as well. Do a three-year comparison of your net worth (see Chapter 5).

Assumption	Challenge/Antidote
My assets have to keep increasing every year.	No, they don't. Assets fluctuate just like the weather. It's the way the world works. *Antidote:* Focus on 10-year periods instead.
Two can live as cheaply as one.	Not really. What happens is that both levels of spending rise to the level of the higher spender in any particular category. *Antidote:* Do a monthly cash flow statement (see Chapter 5) together, and resolve the spending differences that existed between you when you each lived alone.
If others are making a killing, I need to make a killing too.	If you want to have fun risking your money, take a fixed amount and go to Las Vegas. Invest your money in such a way as to make the killing over time.
I need to own my home.	Why? What need does owning address? Is there another way the need could be answered? Maybe your landlord will share the costs of that new hardwood floor.
I know we're rich because we drive a BMW/fly first class/ ski in Aspen/own a boat.	Have you looked at the numbers? The last person who said this to me lost her house to foreclosure a month later.

SPENCER'S SEVEN SIMPLE RULES FOR ACHIEVING MONEY WISDOM

Here are the simple rules that money madness blocks us from following. Once you're cured of your money madness, go back and reclaim these rules as your money wisdom:

1. Pause, take a breath, discuss, and look hard at the numbers before making any financial decision.
2. Spend less than you earn now, not as much as you might earn in the future.
3. Spend mindfully, not mindlessly, and periodically leave the credit cards at home and pay cash instead.
4. Save something—regularly. Give something—regularly.
5. Diversify your investments into many different asset classes.
6. Buy low and sell high. Get aggressive when an asset class is down and act warily when an asset class is up.
7. Realize that your actual net worth far exceeds your bank balance. It includes your talents, your lifetime of future earnings, your family and friends, and your health.

THE CURE FOR
MONEY
MADNESS

INTRODUCTION

Money Madness and Its Cure

Did you ever make an investment because you got a tip from a friend, or because a self-styled Wall Street pundit on cable TV came up with a hot pick?

Ever go in on a time-share or even a summer rental because everybody you knew was doing it, it seemed like a great deal, and you just got caught up in the excitement?

Ever plunk your credit card down on the store counter for something you couldn't really afford—maybe an elegant cashmere sweater or an antique porcelain bowl or a 42-inch high-definition TV—because you believed buying it would make you happy? And heaven knows you deserve such a jolt of happiness given the mood you're in or the day you've had or the fight with your spouse this morning.

Speaking of spouses, have you kept your income a secret from yours? Or what you paid for that jacket you're wearing? Do you have a separate, secret credit card or bank account you haven't bothered to talk about, much less share with your spouse?

If you answered yes to any of these questions, you have money madness.

You know what money madness is, don't you? Of course. You recognize the term because you feel money madness in your own life.

Maybe it's when you look at the mail, see that your monthly bank statement has arrived, and feel a rising tide of anxiety because you really *don't want to know* what the statement says, which is precisely why you feel there are no boundaries on your spending.

Or maybe you sense how money madness has you in its clutches when you pull up to the gas pump in that SUV that once made you feel so masterful, check out the rising price of gas, swallow hard at

1

how you once scoffed at the car's low gas mileage, and experience the sinking sensation that you're a total chump.

Or maybe it's when you can't stop feeling that the size of your house measures the quality of your life—and therefore you're better than your next-door neighbor but way inferior to the guy across the street.

Don't worry. You're not alone. The condition I call money madness is nearly universal.

But here's the good news. Just by acknowledging you have it, you're on your way to the cure and all the rewards of being madness-free.

Those rewards are substantial. Money madness is at the core of all our distress and worry about money, and it keeps us from getting as much money as we could get, living as richly as we might live, and enjoying the wealth we have. Cure your money madness and your distress dissolves. Cure your money madness, and you'll get richer, feel richer, and enjoy the real wealth you have.

Financial how-to won't cure your money madness. There's plenty of financial how-to around—24 hours a day, seven days a week, if we like—in books and magazines, on television and radio, and across the Internet. But money madness undermines our ability to do the how-to. It makes us deaf and blind to the information and advice delivered to us from all those media, on all those channels. The result is that *money madness impairs our income. It undermines our net worth. It deprives us of joy*—not just of joy in the wealth we have but in the life we're living.

So I use the word *madness* deliberately. Your money madness is not just an idiosyncratic quirk; it's unhealthy, and it's harmful. Remember the old saw about the stick-up man offering you the choice of your money *or* your life? Money madness diminishes both. That's why it's time for a cure.

Rational People Behaving Irrationally

Money madness is the irrational behavior that otherwise rational people, like you and me, are driven to when the issue is money.

We can count on the fingers of one hand the number of people who made a fortune overnight by taking a flier on a hot stock tip—and it would probably be four fingers too many. But we're so tempted by the fantasy of instant wealth—of changing our lives overnight—that we'll dip into our savings to try for it. That's irrational; it's acting directly counter to what we know to be the reality—namely, that our chances of getting rich overnight are infinitesimal. It's money madness.

We go in on the time-share deal that all our co-workers or friends or family members are going in on because it's there, because it sounds like an opportunity we can seize effortlessly, because it makes us feel we are getting some kind of advantage we couldn't have gotten otherwise. But it may make absolutely no sense as an investment, and it may make even less sense, financial or otherwise, to be committed to the same vacation in the same place every year. That's madness, too.

We stand at the store counter, our jaws clenched with determination as we almost hurl the credit card down to buy something we don't need with money we don't have. It's what I call an anyway purchase—as in "I'm going to buy it anyway!"—even though it won't really get us the lifelong happiness we're trying to buy, and even though the consequences can be costly. Madness.

We pride ourselves on the openness of our relationship with our spouse—till the spouse asks what we've spent on that new jacket. That's when we shut right down. Money is the great taboo, the place in our lives we don't want anyone else to enter. So our bodies tighten and our mouths are drawn into a thin line, and we close ourselves off from intimacy—which erodes the relationship altogether. It's as if we'd produced the ultimate R-rated movie, *My Money Life*—no one under the age of 100 admitted without a parent.

If that isn't madness, what is?

Money Madness Has Big Consequences

Money madness is everywhere. It shows up in pretty much everyone, and it is as varied and individual as fingerprints.

My friend Steve makes millions and has more credit card debt now than when he made $30,000 a year. Back then, he couldn't pay his bills. He still can't. The reason? He overspends. Now that he earns more than $2 million a year, he overspends on a bigger scale, but the madness is the same: Spend, spend, spend till you're strapped for cash.

I have a client who asked me to double his wealth because he was certain that such a level of wealth would free him from worry and allow him to be happy five years later. I doubled his wealth; he was still worried, still unhappy. "Maybe we could just double it again," he said to me; *then* he'd feel free and be happy.

At a workshop I conducted in Los Angeles in the spring of 2007, just after I announced to the audience of 400 people that it was now "time for everybody to take a good, hard look at the numbers of your own finances," I noticed a commotion in the back of the crowd. A woman was literally having trouble breathing, and a couple of folks nearby were helping her. Even for Southern California, where hyperventilating is practically a way of life, this kind of reaction to the mere idea of confronting your money reality is clearly a kind of madness.

I know a retired single mother of three grown children—all of them highly educated, none of them evidently able to succeed at a job. She has continued to give her kids money until she has little left to support herself in what has become a pretty pinched retirement and what is looking like it's going to be a pretty distressing old age. Think of it as a triple madness—her own self-neglect, supporting her children in their failure rather than helping them succeed, and giving money to gain love.

What's the most famous and fundamental rule of investing? Everyone knows the answer to this: It's to buy low and sell high. In fact, that's the whole point of investing: You buy stock in a company you think shows promise when the price is relatively low. As the company grows and profits, the stock price rises. That's when you sell and pocket the gain—presumably, to reinvest in another low-priced, promising investment. Simple. And, as I say, everyone knows it.

Except, it would seem, the level-headed investment professionals on Wall Street: They routinely violate this famous, fundamental, totally simple rule of investing. As I write this, the stock market is plummeting in value—thanks to continued bleeding from the subprime credit crisis that began in 2007—and investors are selling as fast as they can. Many of those taking their money out of stocks are putting it into gold instead—at the exact moment that the price of gold has hit an all-time high. In other words, they're selling at the bottom and buying at the top of the market—the very opposite of the fundamental investment rule. And this is hardly the first time the pros have acted contrary to their own advice.

Remember the stock market's boom-boom era in the 1990s? That's when Wall Street's wizards climbed onto the technology-stock bandwagon as prices were *rising*, then sold in a panic when the bubble burst in 2000 and prices plunged.

They did the same thing after the terrorist attacks of September 11, 2001, when even the savviest investors sold stocks in huge volumes as fast as they could. The U.S. stock market has trended upward consistently for two centuries despite every form of calamity—civil war, two world wars, panics and recessions and inflations, natural disasters, and even a couple of market crashes. That's history; it is fact; it is there for all to know. Yet when this same stock market reopened the week after 9/11, investors lost their beautifully tailored Savile Row shirts as they sold stocks in a frenzy. Why?

Money madness. History, experience, the facts on the ground all said: Don't sell. The investors did the opposite. It was as if a money monster had them by the throat. The very same money monster who is right now prompting investors to sell stocks at the bottom of the market so they can buy gold at the top of the market, thus squeezing their money two ways. The same money monster who intimidated the Wall Street wizards of the 1990s into buying tech stocks as the price was heading up—lest they fail to ride the rising tide—then frightened them into selling as the stock price plunged—lest they get pummeled in the subsequent downturn. As a result, then as now, the Wall Streeters did both—missed the boom and got caught in the bust.

I've been there. I've felt the adrenaline rush of an up day in the market, the dismal depression of a down day. I have my own money monster driving me to acts of money madness. It put me through years of lunatic money behavior—behavior that, as you'll read, was always foolish, mostly counterproductive, often self-destructive, and on at least one occasion even dangerous. In fact, the money madness it put me through would be downright funny if it weren't so serious.

For make no mistake: Money madness is as bad for our bodies and souls as for our bank accounts and income. It saps our energy and our health, limits our lives, can wreak havoc with our relationships, diminishes our peace of mind, prevents us from enjoying the money we have, and stops us from making more money.

The consequences of money madness are not just harmful, they're painful. Somewhere under that madness, there's a wound that keeps bleeding—as you'll discover in exploring your own money madness. Even the slightest nudge can open the wound, and it hurts.

How much? Have a look at Tony and Ted, old friends who met on the street, hadn't seen one another in a while, and decided to go have coffee and a chat to get caught up. Tony's cinnamon spice mocha took less time to prepare than Ted's half-caf toffee nut latte, so Tony waved to Ted from the cash register and gestured that he was paying for both coffees.

It was a knife in the heart to Ted. First, he sank into shame—Is Tony paying because he thinks I can't afford this? Then he felt suspicion—Is he trying to get something from me? And finally he moved on to resentment—Do I have to pay for him next time? And what if next time isn't coffee but lunch or dinner? It's not fair!

That is a high emotional toll to pay for someone buying you an overpriced cup of coffee. But it is the kind of pain money madness can inflict.

Perhaps most ironically, the money monster excels at helping us lose money; its promises are hollow. The stock tip doesn't make us rich overnight, going in on the time-share requires paperwork and maintenance and attention and empties our wallet, and the thrill we get from buying the 42-inch high-def TV doesn't last. One ball game and we're yearning for the 46-inch screen, or the 52-inch screen, or the 65-inch screen.

"I've been rich and I've been poor," legendary entertainer Sophie Tucker is reputed to have said, "and rich is better."

Well, okay, but she might also have said: "I've been healthy and I've been sick, and healthy is better."

Or "I've had friends and I've had enemies, and friends are better."

Or "I've been in good moods and I've been in bad moods, and good moods are better."

Yet none of these has the *zing!*, the *pow!*, the shock of recognition of the line about money. Nothing else packs the same emotional wallop.

How come? How come you don't feel a need to be cured of your "health madness" or your "friendship madness" or your "mood madness"? Why is it that only the term *money madness* resonates the way it does, nailing the sense we have that a kind of insanity seems to touch everything having to do with money in our lives?

After all, money is nothing more nor less than a medium of exchange—without any intrinsic value itself. Or so the economists tell us. We carry money in our pockets and transact with it passively, automatically: Buy the muffin, pay the toll, slide the debit or credit card across the counter.

Money is neutral—a facilitator. So why is there an epidemic of money madness—and how does the contagion work?

The simple answer is that money madness isn't really about money at all. It's about emotion. It's about intensely subjective feelings that come out of a place very deep within us and go right past the conscious mind as they drive us to act in certain ways. As I learned through years of analyzing and working through my own and my clients' money madness, it starts in childhood, yet it has the power to affect us all our adult lives.

But what if you could free yourself from your money madness? What if you could tame the money monster within you—cool the adrenaline rush you get when you hear the investment tip, not get caught up in the collective rush to a great deal, silence the insistent voice telling you to buy the television?

If you could do that, couldn't you then begin to relate to others on terms of real financial intimacy that might enhance your overall relationship with a spouse or partner—and with friends, relatives, clients, and co-workers as well?

If you could free yourself of your money madness, wouldn't you stop equating money or the things it can buy with happiness, and wouldn't you then also liberate your energies for more joyful living?

If money madness no longer ruled your money behavior, couldn't you keep yourself from losing money—and even make more money?

You could. You can. I did. This book will teach you how.

There's a Cure for Money Madness

My story is in these pages: How I reached a level of money madness that finally brought me up short and sent me searching for a cure. How with help—specifically with the help of noted relationship counselor Anne Watts—I found the cure. How I've been practicing the cure myself and teaching it to others in speeches and presentations, in interactive workshops Anne and I conduct, and on my website at www .curemoneymadness.com. How living a life free of money madness has changed so many lives for the better—my life, my clients' lives, and the lives of workshop participants and of many others.

But the book is your story as well—whatever your current net worth, regardless of your current financial literacy. And one of my goals in writing the book is to show you how a subject often charged with fear and complexity—money—is really simple, once you understand the madness it provokes. Money wisdom doesn't require financial sophistication; in fact, it's better off without it.

That's why awareness is the heart of the cure. To gain it, you'll unveil your own money story, identify your money madness, and confront your personal money monster. You'll inventory the consequences at home, at work, in your personal and business relationships. You'll be asked to assess your financial intimacy quotient, your FIQ, to determine how closely connected financially you and your spouse or partner are, and to understand what this says about your romantic connection as well. You'll come to see what money madness has done to your life and to your net worth.

After that, it's easy. You'll see how to apply your new awareness, helped by some practical strategies I'll offer for organizing your money life in a madness-free way. I'll show you my proprietary Rainbow Portfolio™, an asset allocation strategy for investing that can achieve historically high returns without your lifting a finger—literally.

I'll show you how to get money the madness-free way: how to expel the madness from your work life, how to sell anything, including yourself, and how to ask for money free of all the emotions that hung you up in the past. The result? You'll get more money.

I'll also show you how to spend money the madness-free way, whether you're making the most momentous spending decision most of us make—that is, getting a home—or heading for the mall.

I'll ask you to take another look at your net worth as you calculate your personal definition of enough—that is, what will it really take for you and your family to live the rich life you want to live on a madness-free money track for life? With that, your personal money monster will recede into the background. The striving will end. The madness—and its accompanying distress—will simply melt away.

You'll be richer for it—in every way.

Yes, the cure for money madness asks you some tough questions and puts you through some rigorous exercises. But when you come out the other side, cured of your money madness and freed from your money monster, you will have healed a wound in your life and enhanced your sense of well-being and peace of mind. Your relationships will blossom, your wallet will be decidedly bigger, and you'll be living a life that is more abundant than you ever dreamed.

That's the promise. Are you ready to fulfill it? Let's start by looking more closely at money madness.

CHAPTER 1

Money Madness

What It Does and How It Works

When my wife, Janine, and I first went to see the house in which we now live, the thing that most excited her was the backyard. "Plenty of space for a garden," she said breathlessly. I could see her pleasure as she scanned the sizable expanse of the yard, no doubt already planning vegetables here and perennials there.

The prospect filled me with dread. Where she saw tomatoes on the vine and beds of peonies, I saw bills, expenses, maintenance costs. *If I even acknowledge her pleasure,* I thought to myself, *she'll start planning this garden; and if she does that, I'll have to pay for it.* And if that happened, a lot of money would flow away from me.

"What do you think, Spencer?" she asked me excitedly. "Isn't it just perfect?"

I barely grunted, then looked away. The truth is that I was terrified of spending money on a garden. I was even more terrified of sharing my fear with Janine. It was not something I had ever talked to her about—even though she was and remains the person to whom I feel closest in all the world. So as I always and invariably did, I kept mum, and I simply let my fear simmer.

Irrational? This was sheer folly.

For one thing, we could well afford a garden. Of course, with a packet of seeds you can buy for pennies and a willingness to do a little manual labor, just about anyone can afford a garden. But in fact, our finances at the time would have enabled a professional garden design and help with the heavy-duty work of garden maintenance, so my fear certainly wasn't due to a lack of ready cash.

Nor would it have been rational to reject the garden for the sake of our long-term financial welfare. Quite the contrary. If this became our home and we one day decided to sell it, a garden in the backyard would significantly enhance its resale value.

In fact, by any measure I could possibly come up with, had I been thinking rationally, the garden was a plus. It would give pleasure to my wife—something any husband normally seeks to do. It might provide us with the fresh vegetables I love. If I had allowed myself to think about it, I might have realized that a garden can be a place of relaxation, a place that can refresh the spirit—in short, a "commodity" that might enrich my life.

I yield to few people when it comes to knowing about money. Trained in economics, with an advanced degree in business, certified as a financial planner, I advise some of the wealthiest and most astute investors in the United States. I make a lot of money for them. You don't have to take my word for it. *Worth* magazine has repeatedly named me to its list of the top 100 wealth advisors in the nation.

But standing in the backyard that day, tensing with resistance against the projected outflow of my cash, and seething with resentment at the person I loved most in the world, I was not behaving like a money expert. Rather, my behavior was being driven by money madness.

Fear of money going away from me was one part of the madness, and it was powerful enough to give the boot to all common sense, including financial judgment. Equally telling was my fear of sharing my feelings with my wife. Instead, as Janine and the real estate agent strolled the yard, talking about spring bulbs, summer herbs, and late-fall ornamental grasses, I allowed money madness to create a gulf across which my wife and I were simply not communicating—across which, if truth be told, we never had communicated.

The High Price of Money Madness

Money madness is alive and well at home, in the office, on the factory floor, at play, in the bedroom.

And it has consequences.

I see money madness, and its consequences, in my friend Jack. Jack is not just a captain of industry, he is a brigadier-general. He's the second in command at a prestigious corporation, reporting directly to the supreme commander, the CEO, while an impressive staff of officers and hundreds of worker-troops are Jack's to direct. And so he does, issuing orders and deploying resources with all the confidence of a man in no doubt of his testosterone level or intellectual ability—like Patton on the front lines of the battlefield. Yet when it comes to asking for a raise, money madness takes over, and General Jack crumbles.

Every year, when Jack meets with the CEO for his annual performance review, his personal money monster goes with him. The money monster makes Jack's palms sweaty, dials up his blood pressure, and lowers his normally stentorian speaking voice to a croaking whisper. Instead of asserting his value and declaring what he thinks he's worth, Jack waits for the CEO to tell him he's been a good boy and offer him the reward of a small raise, and Jack's money monster directs him to gush with gratitude for the gift and get out of there as fast as he can.

I see money madness in my neighbors—I'll call them the Smiths—who refuse ever to go into debt. The Smiths' money monster lets them spend only what they have and insists they never borrow, never be beholden to anyone. They're a strictly cash operation.

But they'll also never quite be able to buy a house in which all three kids could have separate bedrooms, and from which the Smiths might some day realize retirement income—simply because saving up that kind of cash could take a lifetime. Instead, they will limit their lifestyle, remaining in their somewhat cramped rental home, where the kids take turns sleeping in the living room, and they will miss out on the opportunity to make an important investment and build financial equity in a house. All for the sake of a belief in the virtue of being debt-free.

The Joneses, by contrast, have made it their life's purpose to do everything for their kids, mortgaging their own present security for their children's future. Despite a consistently rising income, their money monster keeps them overspending endlessly. Result? While the Joneses sweat blood to give their children every advantage, what they're really giving the kids is a model of stress, self-neglect, and poor money management—a legacy that could haunt the younger Joneses for years to come.

I see money madness in my friend Sandy, who bought her house, and overpaid for it, for the fireplace in the living room. She dutifully looked at the other rooms in the house, but the decision had already been made—a function of emotion, not of objective decision-making. Had Sandy really analyzed what the house would cost for repair and maintenance, or assessed whether it might make more financial sense to rent than to buy, she would have seen that it would be a financial struggle for her to own the house, as indeed it has proven to be.

But she didn't do such an analysis. Instead, she saw herself on a cold winter's night, the snow piled high outside, soft music playing, her glass of wine catching the reflection of the fire's flames as she savored the warmth within. Her own personal money monster had drawn the vision for her and kept her focused on it. It was irrational, but it was irresistible—madness at a high price.

Money Madness Comes Between People

Money madness isn't just in us, it's between us. There's a famous story about two women—call them Susan and Sarah—who had been the closest of friends for 20 years.[1] For 20 years, they confided in one another, complained to one another about their husbands, worried about their children, shared secrets. Then one day Susan finally "confessed" to Sarah that she didn't exactly *work* at the art museum, she was on its board of directors and was one of its major contributors, donating to it some of the vast wealth from her trust fund.

It left Sarah not just curious about what else she didn't know about Susan but also wondering who this woman was she'd been telling her innermost secrets to for 20 years. She felt not just distanced but betrayed, and a friendship of 20 years' duration soured irrevocably.

Families can be torn apart by money madness. Mine was. My father's partner in the shoe store he owned was his sister's husband, whom he came to suspect of pilfering from the store cash register. Because my father's money madness was that he couldn't talk about money—a trait I would learn at his knee—he allowed himself to become estranged from his sister rather than solve the issue. Soon, the two families did not speak at all. It wasn't until 37 years later, when all the principals were dead and after I had cured my own money madness, that I was able to hire a private detective and reunite with my first cousins.

I've seen money madness sunder business relationships and ruin business deals. I've seen it undermine sales and anger customers. When I first started out as a financial advisor, I was so reluctant to discuss money that I put off stating my fee till the very end of my sales pitch, then low-balled it so I could get the job. Sometimes it backfired, with a prospective client figuring that if I was promising to deliver all those services for that low fee, I probably didn't know what I was doing.

Money madness is a notorious barrier to intimacy between lovers, spouses, partners. Husbands like me don't let on about the family finances—we just stew over what the garden might cost. Wives tell husbands their new dress cost half its real price. Couples conceal bank accounts or credit cards from one another, thus living separate and secret lives and fostering a kind of lie—while living together. Trust is eroded, communication deteriorates. If you don't know your partner's sense of values, style of dealing with money, definition of abundance, vision of the financial future, can you honestly say you know your partner?

It's Not Irrational When *We* Do It

Here's the real lunacy about Sandy, who bought the house because she fell in love with the fireplace: She's a mortgage broker. She knew her behavior was irrational even as she was doing it.

That is perhaps the single most distinctive characteristic of money madness: It is *behavior we know is totally irrational, except when we do it.*

I knew my behavior was irrational that day in the backyard as I listened to my wife grow increasingly excited over plans for her garden. If clients had been looking at the property and had asked me to offer a financial assessment, I would have extolled the idea of the garden both for its potential enjoyment and for the dollar value it would add. But this wasn't happening to clients or friends; it was happening to me, and the rational me wasn't there to tell the irrational me to cool it.

I also knew I was behaving irrationally by not talking openly to Janine about money. I talked to her about absolutely everything else. I had told her everything there was to know about me—except our assets, my income, our debts, or the money in the family coffers. Three years into our marriage, and I still couldn't discuss those financial basics with my wife.

Yet I always tell my clients that it's essential they talk to their spouses about all financial matters. I've seen what happens when couples don't discuss an investment, or a projected major purchase, or a decision to sell a stock or a property. It isn't just the relationship that suffers; so does the portfolio.

And I knew this. Knew it all implicitly—except when it was happening to me. That was the irrationality. I could be absolutely objective on the subject of the value of gardens and on the need for financial intimacy between spouses, except where my own garden and my own marriage were concerned. That's when objectivity went out the window, rationality didn't stand a chance, and my money madness moved right in and took over.

If I could have seen myself objectively, I probably would have been appalled at my behavior: a grown man, a conscientious breadwinner, a responsible member of the community keeping secrets like a Cold War conspirator. If someone I cared about behaved as I did, I would have done everything in my power to stop him or her. It was only when *I* was behaving that way that I was unable to see how irrational, unwise, and downright unprofitable the behavior was.

Back in the days of the high-tech bubble, my client Bill calmly put 90 percent of his portfolio into a single Internet stock. Certainly, Bill knew—everyone knows—that it is foolish to invest all your wealth in a single stock. That's proverbial wisdom—*Don't put all your eggs in one basket*—even though the value of that one basket had quintupled in a single year and was expected to keep on rising. In fact, had Bill been advising a friend, he would have offered the eggs-and-basket wisdom along with his congratulations.

But as his concentrated portfolio grew in value from $1 million to $2 million to $15 million and more, passing through levels of wealth that once would have seemed to Bill stratospheric but that now seemed sort of normal, he could not say to himself what he would have said to a friend: "Diversify. Allocate your holdings among various assets and distribute your risk." That inability to hear for himself the advice he would have given to another was his money madness. And when the tech bubble burst and the market tanked, Bill's stock went belly-up, and 90 percent of his original wealth was gone.

For most of us, the numbers are smaller, but the principle is the same: The behavior you'd warn a friend to stop, you can't even see in yourself. Someone you care about who is strapped for cash to begin with wants to spend a weekend in Las Vegas, and you sit her down and remind her there are other ways to take a mini-vacation. But *you'll* dip into savings to invest in a get-rich-quick scheme a friend says is a "sure thing."

A pal with a two-star salary starts to pick up the tab at a five-star restaurant. You know that will mean a sacrifice in another arena of the pal's life, so you stop him before he can complete the gesture. But you stand at the store counter determined to take home that overpriced high-def television because *you* want it and it's your due.

That's the money monster at work. In the case of the friend's sure-thing investment, the money monster is the fantasy of having your life change overnight, of being catapulted effortlessly into a realm that is light-years away from your current humdrum existence. You feel it as a sheer physical rush—blood coursing through your veins, heartbeat speeding up.

In the case of the TV, the money monster is that almost indignant sense of merit—the affirming feeling that you're worthy, that your virtuous actions and difficult life experiences have given you a right to the TV, that you're *entitled* to it.

In both cases, an infinitesimal grain of truth injects a note of cruelty into the equation. Yes, it is possible that an investment can so increase in value that your money might double, triple, even quintuple, although probably not overnight. That is indeed possible—in the abstract sense that anything is possible. And certainly you deserve a 42-inch screen—in that same abstract sense that everyone deserves a 42-inch screen. If the universe were pure and rational, both those things would be true.

But that anything is possible and that everybody is deserving, though fine notions, don't really come into play here. The reality of stock market investing is that even a successful investment won't change your life overnight, and an investment tip that promises to do so is very likely an unsound proposition. And everybody knows it.

The reality of consumer spending is that it is a matter of what you can afford, not of inherent or constitutional rights. Everybody knows that, too.

Yet perfectly rational people manage to dismiss these profound and pervasive realities to cling instead to the cruel, infinitesimal grains of truth their private and personal money monsters keep whispering in their ears—"overnight wealth, overnight wealth!" or "you deserve it, you deserve it!" The fact that these same perfectly rational people cannot afford either the stock purchase or the TV is rendered meaningless. It isn't that they don't know they're putting themselves at a disadvantage by spending money they can't afford to spend. Rather, it's that money isn't the issue. The fantasy of life-changing wealth is the issue. The sense of their right to the TV is the issue. The money monster is in charge, and the money monster will not be denied.

It's madness. And if these people saw anybody else buying stocks or TVs they couldn't afford for dumb reasons like these, they would shake their heads and feel sorry for the poor knucklehead.

By the way, after the stock market debacle, I asked Bill how his wife was responding to the loss. His reply astonished me. He had never told his wife about the stock or his investment in it.

"Why not?" I sputtered.

"Because she would have made me sell it," he said.

Of course. Although thoroughly unsophisticated about financial matters, Bill's wife had the kind of common sense he was deliberately and assiduously blocking out. In her simple wisdom, she would have asked if it really made sense to "tie up so much of our money in that one investment." From past experience, she may even have known that Bill had a money monster that made him lose his objectivity—and she would have been prepared to stop him from letting it rule his actions. That's precisely why he didn't tell her. The money monster driving Bill to stick with that stock through yields beyond his wildest dreams was not about to be sidelined by a third party speaking rationally.

It's the reason why today when I meet with clients, I insist on meeting with both spouses; the objectivity of the second spouse—the commonsense wisdom of the financially "unsophisticated"—is absolutely essential. I simply won't do business with them otherwise.

Left to my own devices, I'm not sure my money monster would have let me buy the house we live in today. Fortunately, however, my grumpy disdain for my wife's imagined garden did not prevail. I was able to confront my money monster, saw that my struggle was not with my wife but with my automatic fear of spending money, and overcame the monster's lifelong grip. Today, the garden has become a precious and integral part of our family's life; in fact, I value it more than the house.

By contrast, Bill made sure there would be no chance for his madness to be overturned. He kept it all to himself and allowed his money monster to lead him headlong to disaster without permitting a single rational voice to intervene.

Money Madness Behaviors:
The Top 10

Here are 10 common, irrational money madness behaviors. Do you recognize yourself in one or more of these descriptions? Keep track; these are the behaviors this book will help you cure.

1. **Money Muteness.** You can't talk about money with your spouse. What you spend, how much you earn, what you have in that secret bank account you keep are subjects that are off-limits. When a friend suggests a vacation or restaurant that is way out of your price range, you're tongue-tied. Talking about fees or salary with a client or with the boss is not just uncomfortable, it's downright stressful. You find it far easier—and you're far readier—to talk about sex than about money.

2. **The Prisoner of Spending.** You spend more than you earn even as your salary keeps on going up. You buy things you really don't use and wish you hadn't bought in the first place. You often buy expensive things on impulse. Your credit card is like another bodily appendage; it reacts like a nerve ending. You tend to buy things in bulk, then throw away most of them.

3. **Craving More.** You always think you need more money. Then you get more, and guess what: You need still more. Your "number"—the amount that will be enough, that will finally let you stop craving—turns out to be a moving target that just keeps changing. You become a workaholic to make more money. You hoard and save and buy only the bare necessities. You spend a lot of time fantasizing about how you'll get more money and how your problems will be solved and you'll be free as a bird—just as soon as that amount of money is achieved.

4. **Home Run Hitter.** You're out to make a killing. Now. Making money slowly strikes you as tedious and boring. What you want is the big payoff, the overnight *zap!*, the speculation that keeps you checking the market, biting your nails, feeling the rush. You're not going to miss this ship. Not you. And when you're not checking the market, you're buying the lottery ticket or heading for Atlantic City or Vegas and the potential jackpots there. It isn't money you're really after; it's adrenaline.

5. **Following the Herd.** Just about anyone knows more about money than you do. But there's safety in numbers, as any sheep can tell you. So you watch the talk shows to get financial advice, read the paper, follow the gurus. No need to check out something; if it sounds good on CNBC, or if your friends are doing it, or if your spouse says it's a good idea, you'll do it too. Tech stocks are going up? You're in. It's a recession and everyone else is selling? You too. Hey! If everyone else on the block has a high-def television, then obviously you need to get one too; it would be uncomfortable not to.

6. **Money as Metric.** You measure yourself on the basis of money alone and feel not quite equal to someone who has or earns a lot more or a lot less than you do. It isolates you from friends who aren't doing as well, and it makes you uncomfortable around friends who are doing much better. You're a woman who knows you'll never be able to crack the glass ceiling and make as much as a man. You're a teacher who knows he's stuck at the meager annual salary the state pays. Money means rank, and that's just the way it is.

7. **Money Lying.** Wow! Did you make a killing in the market! Actually, you didn't make quite as big a killing as you say you did, but then, you always exaggerate the truth where money is concerned—whether it's how much you earn, what you spent on your house, how much you save, how much you owe. Some-

times, you exaggerate low, and sometimes, you exaggerate high. But you always exaggerate.

8. **Taking a Siesta.** Who needs numbers? You've got instinct. After all, money isn't the most important thing in the world, so for any major financial decision—buying a car, buying a house, getting a loan, investing—the numbers really don't count all that much, and you don't need to look too closely. It's a part of your life you don't care about, so you can let others handle it for you. Fortunately, you're certain that some divine entity is taking care of things so you can just kick back and watch the money grow on the trees. Whatever.

9. **Money as Weapon.** You're happy to pay for lunch, but you expect something in return—maybe dinner next month? You give your kids money, then tell them how you want it spent: You'll pay for business school but not for social work school. Money is a tool you use to manipulate people.

10. **Money Hatred.** You think money is the root of all evil, and you want it to stay far away from you. Wall Street? The devil's playground—and you won't invest. Rich people? Worthless. Material possessions? Childish toys. If everyone viewed money as you do, the world would be a better place.

The Science Behind Money Madness

What's it all about? Why does money seem to send rational behavior packing? After all, money is numbers—cool, objective, impartial, utterly dispassionate. We *count* money. Money is a matter for calculation. So why does emotion, which is what money madness is really about, trump cool, dispassionate calculation every time?

It trumped counting up the numbers when Sandy bought her

house, determined to live her fireplace fantasy, no matter the cost. It trumped rational behavior when Bill kept playing that one stock over and over, like a gambler hooked on a roulette number seen in a dream. Objective thinking and dispassionate calculation weren't anywhere in sight when Jack went to talk to the CEO about money, or when it took Susan 20 years to admit to having a lot of it, or when I stood in the backyard of my prospective new home and thought about all the money that would flow away from me if we turned the yard into a garden.

Instead, in each case, what ruled was deep-seated, unarticulated emotion. Feelings that invariably and inevitably attach themselves to the whole issue of money. For Sandy, a desire for a comfort and safety she felt were missing in her life. For Bill, virtually the opposite: a sense of control, of power, while taking a great risk. For Susan, shame. For me, fear. Money itself is just the conduit for these emotions, the mechanism through which they are galvanized into action. **Whatever the emotions may be, engaging in a financial transaction stirs them up—and the emotions rule.** Rational, impartial, dispassionate financial calculation doesn't stand a chance. That's money madness.

To be sure, it's hardly news of the man-bites-dog variety that emotion can overrule reason. Where money is concerned, there's even a whole new science to explain exactly how. It's called *neuroeconomics*— the study of the brain activity that takes place when we make economic choices. Neuroeconomists are today imaging the brain and mapping brain waves to monitor what happens physiologically when emotional responses overpower rational thinking in financial decision-making.

This is a very new science, but many of the findings thus far are instructive. For instance, some neuroeconomists studying purchase decisions have found that the desire for instant gratification almost always wins out. Most people would rather have the high-definition television now than sock away the money for retirement in some vague future years from now.

Researchers studying investment decisions found that most people were more averse to loss than they were eager for gain. Presented with a gamble that offers exactly the same odds of winning $150 as of losing $100, people won't bet; they'd rather not risk the loss than take a chance on winning, even though statistically it would be to their advantage to take the chance. They're shown the evidence of that advantage: the cold, hard calculations. But they still fear loss more than they are willing to take even a good chance on gain. Here's neuroeconomic proof that money madness steals your money. It's why learning how to take off the money madness blinders is so essential—so you can confound the neuroeconomists when you confront decisions like these and keep what your money madness would steal.

The Money Monster in My Throat

It steals more than money. Energy, intimacy, joy, peace of mind, even physical health are all adversely affected when the money monster is governing your behavior and driving you to acts of money madness.

I felt my money monster as I stood in the garden that day, distancing myself from my wife and her garden dreams. It didn't feel good. I experienced all the physical manifestations of fear. I was a little shaky, my throat felt tight, my forehead was tensed, I didn't think my voice would work right, my breathing was shallow, and my heart was pounding. What was I so afraid of?

The answer is simple: To me, money was security. Money was safety. Money was really nothing less than survival. Therefore, there could never be enough money, what there was must be tightly gripped, and no one else must ever, ever know how much or how little of it I had. That is why what looked like a garden to my wife looked to me like a threat to my safety and security and, in a very real sense, to my survival. No wonder my heart was pounding.

Where did the fear come from? How did it get there? How did it turn into a money monster driving me to such money madness? Turns out it all started long ago. In the next chapter, you'll see the evolution of your money madness too.

CHAPTER 2

Contracting the Condition

How We Get Money Madness

How do you get money madness? It starts with money messages we receive in childhood, long before we understand what money is all about and what role it plays in life. All we understand is the feeling that the money message is attached to; that's what makes the impact, and that's what stays with us. Later on, engaging with money causes us to revisit the moment when we received the childhood money messages—and to relive the moment's emotional impact. The resulting behavior is money madness.

And the truth is these childhood money messages are transmitted to us all the time, in all sorts of ways.

Maybe we overhear our parents' whispered worrying about money. We intuit their anxieties about paying the bills, and it erodes our sense of safety. We take on the anxious feelings for ourselves without really understanding the why or wherefore.

Or maybe we hear our parents arguing about money in raised voices, accusations flying back and forth. We feel the distrust between them and are cowed by the expressions of anger. It's frightening.

The next-door neighbors get a brand-new car or renovate their kitchen with granite countertops or one of them gets promoted to vice president with a corner office, and our parents wallow in envy and a bit of self-pity. What's emotionally charged for them is emotionally charged for us; we follow their feelings in this as in most things, and we get a message about what money—and its lack—can do.

We grow up in a home where money is treated with cavalier indifference. Our parents spend freely, and if they get into debt, assume "it will work out." We absorb a sense of carelessness—even inattention—where money is concerned. It breeds a blasé attitude: The message is there are no consequences, no cause-and-effect relationships, when money is the issue.

The messages affect us in much the same way that sensory stimuli reach infants. Like infants, we don't understand them in any rational or intellectual sense. But like sensory stimuli, they keep coming at us from our environment. **Those that reach us on waves of emotion— sometimes through some form of dramatic initiation, sometimes through the gradual accumulation of impressions—are the most powerful, and they eventually form our perception of money: Money is security, or it's divisive, or it's the thing we measure ourselves by.**

Those messages imprint themselves onto our psyches, and that imprinted memory, with its ability to replay the emotions of childhood, is the money monster of the process. Later in life, when we engage with money in some way, the money monster is stirred into action, and the powerful childhood emotion comes flooding back—often with an intensity that quickens our senses in an almost electrifying way.

Money Madness Hurts

As the conduit of our childhood emotions and the instigator of our adult money behavior, the money monster is a diligent demon. He sits right on our shoulder so he can whisper money madness into our ear and rule our money behavior. He drives our behavior by making us feel that a higher salary can slake our fears and anxieties, that buying the sports car will compensate for our inadequacies and weaknesses, that investing in that stock our dentist's brother-in-law recommended will fulfill our fantasies.

It's painful. It hurts as a grown-up to feel again the anxiety, fear, confusion, melancholy, resentment—all the emotions that the world of money caused us to feel as children.

And the money monster's presence on our shoulder is also a weighty burden. Those childhood emotions don't just rule our money behavior; they confine us. We think we're acting like responsible adults, but we're actually limited in our range of motion. Anxiety, fear, confusion, melancholy, resentment don't strengthen capability; they erode it. The money monster takes charge, and he's got us on a leash.

And he is greedy, always hungry for more. "More will fill the emptiness!" he constantly tells us. But the truth is that the more you feed the money monster, the hungrier he gets.

So there we are, all grown up, with our jobs, our houses, our families, our investment portfolios—and driven to childish behavior where money is concerned. By now, however, by adulthood, we're comfortable with our money monsters. They've been with us so long they're almost like old acquaintances; we might not recognize our life without them. We've never questioned our childhood money messages; we've never challenged our money monsters. We don't even know there's a wound there—the original childhood pain that created the money monster in the first place.

Find your childhood money message, and you can confront the money monster and identify the wound. Heal the wound and you tame the money monster. And when that happens, you'll be free to live a truly rich life.

My Money Initiation

It took a major fire for me to see the light on this issue.

I remember that it was a Tuesday, the first day back to work after the long Memorial Day weekend. Philadelphia had just suffered one of its most severe winters, so the "official" start of summer was a welcome event, and the weather was indeed warm and pleasant.

Not that I took any particular notice of the weather. Or of the holiday weekend for that matter.

I was 27 years old, a recent graduate of Wharton Business School, and at work at my first job—financial advisor and marketing manager in a large and well-known Philadelphia investment firm. *Hard* at work. Hard like the legendary stock market go-getters of the bull market in the 1990s. Hungry for success. Ready to measure that success in the money I made for others, which was how I made money for myself.

So I put in 12- and 14- and 16-hour days. I went without sleep, skipped meals, was the first to arrive at the office in the morning, and rarely left till night had fallen, even in the long, light-filled days of late May. When I had a date, I'd come back to the office after taking the woman home so I could work some more. Sometimes, I left the office as my boss was arriving for work.

I went after all the leads, read all the research reports, dutifully executed all the transactions. I also compiled lists of new prospects, created in-depth customer profiles, monitored deals, and generated endless reports of trades executed. I was passionate, focused, single-minded—a comer.

The fire that Tuesday started in the ninth floor records room. It spread quickly, consuming tons of paper documents that fueled its heat to 2,000°F. The building was evacuated; 1,500 of us marched out in good fire-drill form. Then the city's firefighters poured more than 12 million gallons of water onto the blaze. The water cooled the fire, then quenched it, then flooded down from the ninth floor to the second floor where the brokerage offices were located, soaking—and thereby destroying—computers, printers, scanners, cartridges, files, tapes, disks.

I panicked. *My records!* I thought. *My lists of prospects! My customer profiles! Deal reports! Transaction data!* They were the tools of my trade. Their destruction, as I saw it, meant the destruction of my livelihood.

I was a nervous wreck. I wouldn't be able to learn the fate of all the hard-earned, hard-won information in my files till morning—if then. I had to do something, so I spent the evening going from door to door in my neighborhood, trying to sell financial services. "Hi, I'm Spencer Sherman," I would begin. "I live up the street, and I'd love to talk with you about growing your money." I rang more than 40 doorbells. One trusting soul, who may simply have felt sorry for me, actually agreed to let me invest his IRA. The rest probably thought there was a madman on the block.

In the morning, I raced back to my office. Blue-uniformed police officers barred my way. The fire was still smoldering; arson was suspected; a reward had been posted. The officials manning the still-chaotic site were jittery. The atmosphere was tense.

I babbled that retrieving my documents from the doomed building was a matter of life or death. One sympathetic cop allowed me to pass. I headed up to the second floor, up to my knees in water, splashing through garbage and downed wires. It was dumb and dangerous, but I was oblivious to those facts and everything else as I reached my office and grasped my livelihood in my hands.

The computer was a goner—saturated and dead. My paper files had all been drowned, but I jammed them soaking wet into my knapsack, which now weighed as much as a stack of gold ingots, and raced for home.

My house had a small, fenced-in plot of lawn out back. I meticulously separated the dripping-wet papers and spread them, one by one, across the lawn to dry.

It was useless, of course. The writing on the papers might as well have been done in disappearing ink. That afternoon, I tiptoed among the sun-dried pages—the papers I had "saved" as if they were the singular totems of a primal religion—and noted that every single one of them was blank.

That's when it hit me. *What on earth am I doing?*

I stopped. I simply stopped in my tracks. And what had started out as the worst day of my life began turning into the best. In that moment, I saw for the first time my own money madness and what it was doing to me. The fire had done more than burn up paper; it had illumined a profound truth about my behavior around money—actually, about all human behavior around money.

Barefoot on my back lawn, I witnessed my own crazy behavior. I saw myself as I must have appeared to others. As I clearly did appear to my neighbors, to the sympathetic policeman who let me enter the still-smoking building, to the colleagues I had called, and to the clients who had called me *to ask if I was all right*—not to ask whether they had lost their money. Of course they hadn't. Data about such transactions are backed up any number of times in computers located outside the city and equipped with every form of recovery program.

I was young, fit, and vigorous. In no way was my career over or my livelihood destroyed. Yet that's exactly how I was behaving. Zigzagging among the blank sheets of paper, I must have looked like a character in a madcap comedy. My behavior was not just illogical, it was ludicrous.

There was nothing I could do except acknowledge what I was feeling. And what I was feeling was fear. *What am I so afraid of?* I asked myself.

My Childhood Money Message

The answer was there instantly, springing up from my memory in sharp focus. It took me from my grown-up home in Philadelphia back to my childhood and into my family's modest apartment in Queens, New York.

I am eight years old. It is evening, after dinner. I am standing in the narrow galley kitchen of the apartment, and my father is seated at the table. That day, my pals and I have been talking about money; some of the guys have confided—boasted!—what their fathers do for a living and how much money they make. So as children of that age do, I ask my father how much money he makes.

My father does not answer. He just stares at me—a cold look of barely suppressed fury.

Do I understand the message in his eyes? You bet I do. Not in so many words—no child of eight could possibly articulate the impact of such a stare. But I know what it says.

It says: Keep out! It says: Back off! You have approached a high-voltage wire that is dangerous and absolutely off-limits! It says: Shh! Money is the key to our survival; don't even speak of it. Ever. To anyone.

What I felt was a two-pronged hammer blow that stunned and frightened me. *Pow!* Shame. *Bam!* Fear. Even mature adults aren't too good at dealing with shame and fear. For a kid, the whole thing was simply beyond my ability to understand, much less cope with.

I responded as any child would. In the parlance of psychology, I internalized the hammer blow. That childhood message about money—*Do not enter! Danger! Quiet! Money means everything!*—was almost literally stamped into my subconscious, imprinted onto my psyche. And my personal money monster began to take shape.

Money Messages Keep Playing for Life

Money is security. You can never have enough money. And you must never speak of it to others.

That's the message I received that evening in our kitchen in

Queens, my initiation into the money taboo. From that moment on, the meaning of the message stayed with me; it would drive my actions where money was concerned for a long time to come.

In my case, the initiation was dramatic: The money message was imprinted onto my psyche in a moment as searing as the fire that 20 years later would finally prompt me to question the message. But eight-year-olds don't question most messages they receive from their parents. We especially don't question the childhood *money* messages we receive, because we simply don't have the knowledge, objectivity, or wherewithal to do so.

Think about it: What's money when you're a kid? It's a treat from the ice-cream truck. It's a doll or a toy or a game for the Xbox. It's the new car that Mommy and Daddy have decided they can't afford. It might even be something Mommy and Daddy complain you don't understand the value of, and you don't. Money is *things*—and beyond that, it's pretty abstract.

Because of that—because as kids we just don't get what money is—our childhood money messages tend to be distorted perceptions. After all, they are formed in emotion and refracted through feeling— the pleasure of the treat or toy, the down feeling you intuit about the new car, the hurt when you're told you don't know the value of a dollar. Rational interpretation doesn't have much to do with the process.

Instead, the emotion imprints itself within us, giving rise to a money monster that lurks in our psyches, ready to haul out the defining emotion of the past to regulate our money behavior in the present. Thus do the money messages we receive in childhood continue to affect us as adults.

That evening in the kitchen wasn't the only time I heard my childhood money message, although it was clearly one of the most formative, because it came back in a flash on the day I was able to see my money madness in action for the first time. The message—*Money is security, you can never have enough, you must never talk about it*—was all around me. It did not need to be articulated; it was part of the fabric of my life.

When we went out to the neighborhood restaurant for dinner, my father would always wear an old, almost threadbare jacket, never the new, dark blue coat my mother always urged him to wear. The message there was: Why should our neighbors know we're doing well enough that I can afford a new jacket? The message seeped through to me via my feelings of embarrassment: *Never let anyone know your money situation. If it's good, people will try to get the money from you, so be watchful where money is concerned. Be wary. Be afraid.*

When we would drive into Manhattan for a visit to a museum on a Sunday, my father always refused to "waste money," as he said, on a parking lot or garage. Instead, we would drive around and around the city blocks in search of an elusive free parking space—endlessly, as it seemed to my sister and me. For me, every minute spent searching ticked away the time I would have to explore the treasures of the museum—the dinosaur, the dioramas of life in ancient times when mastodons roamed the earth, the planetarium. To a child, such a loss of pleasure is momentous, and it became a further lesson for me in the profound importance of money, which was powerful enough to direct our lives down to the smallest detail.

This sense of the importance of money permeated my childhood, carefully recorded every step of the way by my money monster—the sense that money was so profoundly essential it couldn't even be discussed, as if words couldn't measure its significance or the power of its consequences. That's why it was such a secret, and that's why the secret had to be guarded so closely.

As I grew to adulthood, the money monster reliably showed up for every money decision, increasingly dictating my responses to money and my behavior where money was concerned. Always, I turned inward, clammed up, and held tight to what I had earned even as I worked hard to build my money fortress higher and thicker.

So it was probably not surprising that I chose a career in money: because I saw money as key to my survival and my identity. Nor was it surprising that I found it so difficult to discuss fees with a prospective client—or to talk about money at all. When I first met Janine, I was completely at ease discussing my sexual history in detail on our second date, but talk about money—values, goals, dreams, debts, possessions, assets? You've got to be kidding!

Awareness Is the Cure

The cure for your money madness starts with awareness. And the first step to awareness is to go back to your childhood to find the money messages transmitted to you when you were a little kid. Understand how you contracted your madness, and you're halfway to curing it. Maybe more than halfway.

Some people know their childhood money message the instant they hear the phrase "childhood money message." "Oh yes," they say with the shock of recognition, "my childhood money message was that money is security" or "money is meaningless" or "money is evil" or "money is a subject we simply do not talk about."

Some people received their money message in the kind of dramatic initiation I underwent. Or they know it in their bones, like my friend Victor, a clergyman's son, who grew up in a home where money was never talked about, was rarely spent on anything but necessities, and was mostly given away to charity. Victor absorbed his childhood money message loud and clear—"Money is alien, not something to value, not something that ought to have anything to do with you"—even though not a word was spoken.

But others have to search for their childhood money message, and the memory may be reluctant to surface or hard to recognize. After all, what you are looking for is a distorted perception about money that was planted in your brain—with considerable emotional force—when you were young. It's not necessarily going to be easy to spot.

Go On, Recite Your Family's Money Mantra

Let's start by looking at parental mantras—favorite pieces of money wisdom that our parents delivered with seemingly benign purpose. These mantras often reflect your particular culture or background, economic class, or even your parents' political philosophy. If you grew up a coal-miner's daughter with a strike box in the kitchen, the mantras your parents delivered were probably not the mantras picked up by the child of a corporate vice president who collected a monthly paycheck and a gold watch on retirement.

My father's mantra was about success. "To measure your success," he used to say, "count your bank balance." He said it so often that I hear his voice whenever my bank statement arrives in the mail, or when I take a day at the beach and do something that I know *can't* be measured in dollars—a tribute to the power of the parental scoreboard.

My mother's mantra was "We can't afford it," and that pretty much ended the conversation. Often, when I'm shopping, I push against that boundary.

What were your parents' mantras about money? Write them down here. Don't probe too deeply for now; just write down the first things that come into your mind, the sayings about money your father and mother could be relied on to deliver:

My father's money mantra was

_____

My mother's money mantra was

_____

Which Money Maxims Ring True for You?

Maybe the loudest way money messages come to us is in the form of all those money maxims—standard aphorisms about money that we hear constantly: Money doesn't grow on trees. Marry rich. Neither a borrower nor a lender be. If you got it, flaunt it. The love of money is the root of all evil.

They come from many sources—religion and the Bible, folk sayings, Madison Avenue, song lyrics, even from Shakespeare. They are heard so often they have become clichés, cultural norms we don't have to think about; they're just in the air.

When we are children, these maxims are tossed at us like pacifiers. But they reflect the beliefs and values of those who do the tossing— our parents, teachers, and religious leaders—typically, people in authority over us. So the maxims represent a standard of behavior that we understand is admired or approved by the people we admire and whose approval we seek. And that makes them very powerful indeed, clichés or not.

Still, some resonate with us more than others, and by isolating those that trigger a response in us, we can get a further clue into the forces that shaped our own money message.

Here's an exercise I call Adopt-A-Maxim. Read the list of 50 money maxims below, and put a check mark next to those that trigger some sort of emotional response in you. It doesn't matter where that emotion comes from—home, school, friends—if the saying hits a chord, check it.

Adopt-A-Maxim

Maxims	✔
Money isn't everything.	
Keep your assets liquid.	
I'm not made of money.	
The more you have, the more you want.	
Don't talk about money.	
You're only as good as your last sale.	
Daddy works hard to make that money.	
Take what you get and be glad of it.	
Money doesn't grow on trees.	
There's plenty more where that came from.	
You can't take it with you.	
Money corrupts.	
Don't trust people with money.	

Maxims	✔
Time is money.	
Money is power.	
A penny saved is a penny earned.	
The only things certain are death and taxes.	
No money, no honey.	
God will provide.	
Don't tell your mother/father what it cost.	
You get what you pay for.	
Money comes with strings attached.	
It takes money to make money.	
Rent, don't buy. That way, you're not responsible when the roof caves in.	
Paying rent is just throwing money down the drain.	
Do something you love, and it will all work out.	
Money can't buy happiness, but it lets you choose your own form of misery.	
Appear to have more money than you have.	
You must own your own home.	
Money is safety.	
Earn your own money.	
If you marry for money, you end up working for it.	

Maxims	✔
Property is theft.	
Stay out of debt.	
God helps those who help themselves.	
Give and you shall receive.	
You can marry more in a minute than you can make in a lifetime.	
Money is there for the taking; go get it.	
Never buy retail.	
There is no such thing as a free lunch.	
I've been rich and I've been poor, and rich is better.	
The meek shall inherit the earth.	
Spend for quality; it will last longer.	
Money equals happiness.	
You can't be too thin or too rich.	
Money talks.	
Money makes the world go around.	
You can't buy love.	
It is easier for a camel to pass through the eye of a needle than for a rich man to enter heaven.	
It's only money.	
Total number of check marks	

What do you see in the results? Do the money maxims that ring a bell for you focus on one aspect of life more than on others—on consumption perhaps or on choosing how to make a living? That's a hint about the gravitational force pulling you toward your particular money behavior.

Note also the maxims that have no emotional sting as far as you're concerned—the ones with no check mark. What do they seem to focus on? Consider that there are people for whom these sting-free maxims do warrant a check mark. If they're not touched by what touches you, and you're not affected by what affects them, then isn't it reasonable to assume that the messages have no intrinsic validity but are conduits for your personal monster? Note down what it feels like to be made aware of an entirely different money reality.

The Money Message That Scores a Direct Hit

Maybe none of these maxims scored a direct hit on your emotions. So let's dig a little deeper. This exercise asks you to complete three thoughts. Keep answering till you have nothing left to say:

I hate money because . . . [Examples: I never have enough. It's hard to get. It defines who I am.]

_____

_____

_____

I love money because . . . [Examples: I can buy almost anything on the Internet today. It makes my life easy. It makes people look up to me.]

_____

_____

_____

Money is . . . [Examples: Evil. What makes the world go around. Something no one should talk about.]

_____

_____

_____

Take a look. Your statements should give you some inkling as to how you feel about money. That's a good clue to your childhood money message.

You can find another clue by exploring your adult behavior. Here's an exercise for doing so. Below are 20 statements that get at some common money behaviors and feelings. While few such statements are either entirely true or purely false, answer what you mostly believe or what is mostly true for you:

Me and My Money

Statements	True	False
I need a new car every three years.		
Investing is exciting.		
I can't be bothered to balance my checkbook.		
My retirement plan is my house.		
In my neighborhood, it's important to keep up with the Joneses.		
I'd like to be earning more, but I don't know how to ask for a raise.		
When I'm out with friends, I'm often the one who picks up the check at the restaurant.		
When I'm out with friends, I often say up front that we all need to pay our own way at the restaurant.		
I have a fear of turning into a homeless street person.		

Statements	True	False
I find it impossible to save money.		
I simply can't afford a vacation this year.		
I'm an impulse buyer.		
My credit card debt is off the charts.		
I would never charge interest on a loan to a friend or family member.		
Money can't buy happiness, but it makes a good down payment on it.		
Somebody's going to win the lottery; it could just as easily be me.		
My spouse/partner doesn't really know all there is to know about my net worth.		
I'm sometimes embarrassed to have more money than my friends.		
I'm sometimes embarrassed to have less money than my friends.		
Putting away money for retirement each month is my religion.		

What hint do the statements that ring true with you provide about the childhood money messages that were transmitted to you? What do they tell you about the emotional response money provokes or awakes in you? Can you characterize the emotions these responses evoke? In the following list, put a check mark next to each emotion that's applicable.

Emotional Responses

Emotion	✔
Anger	
Worry	
Pleasure	
Paralysis	
Fear	
Excitement	
Obsession	
Challenge	
Introspection	
Generosity	
Focus	
Dreaminess	
Indifference	
Shame	
Joy	
Anxiety	
Numbness	
Other (specify)	

Okay. Why did you mark *those* emotions? Go as far back as you can to the original punch of feeling. Now, tell or write down a story from childhood associated with that feeling. As you do the telling or the writing, note in the table below what feelings the story brought forth when it happened and what feelings the retelling of it brings forth now.

History of Emotions		
The Story	**What I Felt at the Time**	**What I Feel Now**

What is the single, strongest message you take away from this writing or discussion exercise? Write it down.

My Childhood Money Message

That's your childhood money message. This is the force that gave birth to your personal money monster and that continues to affect your money behavior today. In the next chapter, you'll explore just how the monster affects your behavior—in all aspects of your life.

CHAPTER 3

Money Madness in Action

How the Money Monster Operates in Your Life

One day in the gym, I overheard a conversation between a woman and her personal trainer. Their session was over, and they were taking a break, and the client, a bit sweaty and still a bit out of breath, enthused to her trainer: "While I don't really see any change in my body yet, I just know that by working out with you like this twice a week, I'm bound to see dramatic change six months from now!"

But the trainer shook her head. "Sixty percent of your body shape derives from what you eat," she said. "You can work out with me seven days a week, but if you don't deal with that fundamental, any change in your body will be minimal, cosmetic, and temporary."

It's the same with money. You can make all the right moves and do all the smart money tasks outlined in any number of sound, sensible financial books, but if you don't tame your money monster, you'll still pay the price for your personal money madness. Follow the suggestions of David Bach and Suze Orman—and I highly recommend you do so, because they both know their stuff—and you'll start growing your equity and diminishing your debt, and it will all make you feel better. But if your money monster is still alive and well and governing your money behavior, all of it will have only "minimal, cosmetic, and temporary" effect. The first time the monster raises its head, you'll just backslide to square one.

I've seen it a million times. The reckless overspender manages to squirrel enough away to qualify for a mortgage and buy a house, and she feels great about it. And so she should: She's shown herself to be financially responsible, she's made a smart investment, and she's on her way to having some equity. So she goes to the home improvement warehouse in the mall and starts spending as recklessly as she always used to—in credit card debt again!—because her money monster is still calling the shots.

I've seen it in myself as well. You might have thought that the fire at my job in Philadelphia would have cured me of my money madness, but it didn't. It showed me my madness in action, and it led me back to the memory of my childhood money message. But I still hadn't come to terms with my money monster, much less tamed it. And so, like anyone who hasn't had that confrontation, I backslid—right back to working as hard as I could to gain more money and have even more security.

I had eagerly accepted an offer to work in Citibank's private banking division in New York. The train ride from Philadelphia to New York in those days was a little under two hours. Add in the time to get to and from home or office and the train station, and you're talking about a good four hours of commuting time every day. As I was still putting in endless hours on the job—lest I miss out on another possible penny of earnings—that meant a pretty punishing schedule. It wasn't at all unusual for me to get up at 4:00 A.M. so I could just make the 5:15 A.M. train, work hard all day, grab the 9:05 P.M. back to Philly, and arrive home at eleven at night—just in time to catch a few hours of sleep before rising again at four.

One cold winter's night when I had indeed been awake since four, had put in a grueling day at the office, and was racing through New York's Penn Station to catch my train back to Philadelphia, I saw some homeless men huddled in a corner of the station, wrapped in grimy blankets, asleep. I envied them. The thought flashed through my mind: *They're the rich ones; they can sleep.* I, by contrast, was so exhausted my body was ready to drop—except that my money monster kept pushing my body forward, demanding more! more! more! all the time.

I had all the financial skills a person could want. I had done the smart planning and savvy asset allocation and intelligent investing. But all of that was beside the point because I was on a treadmill: No matter how much more money I gained, by definition, it could never be enough; I had to keep moving. Each upward notch on my personal money scoreboard was a signal to the money monster to urge me to get more. So I kept driving myself, living a life consumed by work, with little time for friends, for recreation, or for creating a family—much less enjoying one.

I knew this was madness, but that's all I knew. The lesson I still hadn't learned was this lesson I now pass on to you:

Unless and until you identify your childhood money message, confront your money monster, and deal with the emotions money stirs in you, all the savvy personal finance moves in the world will take you only so far. You still won't be living as richly as you might, you still won't be able to feel peace of mind and real joy about all the wealth you possess, and you still won't be gaining as much money as you could—no matter how good your financial plan and how neatly you've allocated your assets.

So in this chapter, you'll profile your money madness in action to see just how your money monster operates. We'll start at the end. It sounds counterintuitive, but think about it: To find your money monster, it makes sense to examine the behavior it causes.

Catch Your Money Madness in Action

You're about to answer questions about your behavior in 10 categories of life in which money has an impact. Six of the categories are obvious; they *sound* like money: spending, investing, saving, giving, working, doing business. The other four don't sound like money at all—home, friends, family, and love life. But these too are arenas of life in which money is important and that therefore stir money behavior on your part. Put them all together, and these 10 categories can draw a comprehensive picture of your money life. It's a picture that will show you your money madness in action.

These questions do not make up a test. You won't end up with a score. Nor do the questions constitute a competition. You cannot win or lose. Answer yes or no to each, and note if the question itself sparks an emotional response and whether that emotional response has a physical manifestation. For example, do you feel short of breath, do your muscles tense, or do you feel your posture slump at the question?

Track every response no matter how small it seems. Ignore even the slightest discomfort as too minor to bother with, and you may literally be diminishing your potential for wealth.

Ditto for digging deep on this exercise: Honest answers make you money; dishonest answers keep you where you are.

So, begin.

Tracking Your Money Madness Behavior: Spending			
Questions	Yes	No	Emotional/Physical Response
1. Do you find that you rarely use your big-ticket purchases—maybe the new boat, or the 21-speed bike, or the gas barbecue grill with infrared rotisserie?			
2. Have you ever bought anything in order to impress others?			
3. Do you shop as an antidote to depression?			
4. Is spending money stressful—especially on a big purchase?			
5. Do you use credit cards or borrowed money when you shop?			
6. In a casino or at the racetrack, if you exceed your gambling limit, do you keep on playing so you can win your money back?			
7. Is your credit card debt increasing as your income rises?			

Tracking Your Money Madness Behavior: Investing

Questions	Yes	No	Emotional/Physical Response
1. Do you turn up the volume on the radio or TV when the stock market report is broadcast?			
2. Do you buy high and sell low?			
3. Ever invest on a tip from a friend?			
4. Ever invest on a tip read in a magazine article?			
5. How about on a tip you overheard somewhere?			
6. Is your money doubling, on average, every 5 to 10 years?			
7. Are you looking for an investment home run—a huge win that will change your life?			
8. Do you worry about the market?			
9. Does worry about the market sap your energy?			
10. Do you ever lose sleep worrying about your investments?			
11. Do you pay no attention to your investments and have no idea how they're doing?			
12. Do you avoid investing because you can't tolerate the market fluctuations?			

Tracking Your Money Madness Behavior: Saving

Questions	Yes	No	Emotional/Physical Response
I. Is there never enough left over for you to save?			
2. Are your accumulated savings sacred to you—that is, you won't touch this money except in an emergency, and even then only reluctantly?			
3. Are you saving for a purpose?			
4. Do you dip into your savings to pay for things other than the intended purpose?			
5. Is it stressful not to have any savings?			
6. Is it stressful to have savings?			
7. Are you reluctant to start an automatic savings plan?			

Tracking Your Money Madness Behavior: Giving

Questions	Yes	No	Emotional/Physical Response
I. Do you give out of obligation?			
2. Do you give out of guilt?			

Questions	Yes	No	Emotional/Physical Response
3. Do you give for the tax write-off?			
4. Do you give primarily to those organizations that solicit your charity?			
5. Do you give strategically—on the basis of what you want to do in the world or how to change the world?			

Tracking Your Money Madness Behavior: Working

Questions	Yes	No	Emotional/Physical Response
1. Are you earning what you are worth?			
2. Are you able to ask for a raise?			
3. Do you work extra hours to please the boss?			
4. Is fear keeping you in your present job?			
5. Do you distance yourself from people making more or less than you?			
6. Do you "pad" your expense account?			

Questions	Yes	No	Emotional/Physical Response
7. Do you ever take office supplies or other items from work?			
8. Do you live for the weekends—and are you working for retirement?			

Tracking Your Money Madness Behavior: Doing Business

Questions	Yes	No	Emotional/Physical Response
1. Do you state your price or fee up front?			
2. Do you overcharge?			
3. Do you undercharge?			
4. Do you overpromise to make the sale or do the deal?			
5. Do you underpromise to keep the price or fee low so that you'll look good when you deliver more?			
6. Do you avoid difficult conversations—with an upset client, an angry supplier, an unhappy employee?			
7. Is your staff well paid?			

Tracking Your Money Madness Behavior: Home			
Questions	**Yes**	**No**	**Emotional/Physical Response**
1. Can you afford your home?			
2. Has your home become more a burden than a pleasure?			
3. When you come home and walk through the door, do you feel relaxed?			
4. Do you justify your spending on the house—mortgage, maintenance, etc.—with this mantra: "I'll get it back when we sell"?			
5. Do you have a cushion or contingency fund to cover any problem with the house—replacing the roof, for example?			
6. Did you buy your house as an investment?			
7. Has moving to a new home required upgrading your lifestyle—at a cost you had not anticipated?			

Tracking Your Money Madness Behavior: Friends

Questions	Yes	No	Emotional/Physical Response
1. Are you at ease with friends who have significantly more money?			
2. What about with friends who have significantly less money?			
3. Do you hide the truth of your financial situation?			
4. Have you ever loaned money to a friend out of guilt or obligation?			
5. Can you discuss your money fears with your friends?			
6. Have you ever borrowed money from friends—or would you consider asking a friend for a loan?			

Tracking Your Money Madness Behavior: Family

Questions	Yes	No	Emotional/Physical Response
1. Have you chosen to provide some form of financial assistance to your adult children—maybe including them in the family cell phone plan or "helping" with a down payment for housing?			

Questions	Yes	No	Emotional/Physical Response
2. Have you discussed finances with your aging parents?			
3. Do you loan or give money to family members out of guilt or obligation?			
4. Does your financial assistance to family members burden you financially?			
5. Do you find it stressful to provide financial assistance to family members?			
6. Have you ever asked for financial assistance from family members—or would you consider doing so if you were in need?			

Tracking Your Money Madness Behavior: Love Life

Questions	Yes	No	Emotional/Physical Response
1. Do you conceal money matters from your partner?			
2. Are you able to have a calm, productive, blame-free conversation about money with your partner?			
3. Does your partner know your dreams of the future—the ones that might cost money?			

Questions	Yes	No	Emotional/Physical Response
4. Do you know what your partner earns, spends, invests, saves, gives away to charities or causes?			
5. Do both of you know each other's debts—and the facts about any joint debt?			
6. Have you ever withheld sex to counter your spouse's withholding of money or because you're angry at the way your spouse handles money?			
7. What about vice versa? Have you ever withheld money to counter your spouse's withholding of sex?			
8. Does your partner really know all your money secrets? I mean *really*.			

What do the answers tell you? Do you see a profile of your money madness? Try describing it here.

My Money Madness

Money Madness in the Body

I hope you were careful to note down any physical reactions to the questions about your money behavior, because it's absolutely typical for money madness to manifest itself in the body.

In my case, I used to feel it in my heartbeat, my gut, and my voice. At the height of my madness, a stock tip overheard on the street would send a rush of adrenaline through my body. My heart would speed up, and I'd feel a kind of anxious fear in the belly. *Gotta bet on this*, my body would be saying. *If I don't, I'll miss out. I'll be a jerk.*

In a meeting with a prospective client, my throat would tighten as I approached the moment when I would state my fee. As I actually spoke the dollar figure, the pitch of my voice would rise and the volume would go down, almost as if someone else had stepped in to ask for the money. This was fear, of course—fear that the client would balk at my price and turn me down, plus the old childhood fear of talking about money.

In the workshops Anne Watts and I run, people tell us how they can feel their hearts speed up and their bodies tense with anticipation when the market report comes on the radio or television. If their stocks have gone up, their bodies seem almost to stretch with the news; if it has been a down day, their bodies shrink back. That's the money monster at work.

Many participants have told us they have trouble looking wealthier people in the eye. That's the money monster telling them that since they have less money, they have less self-worth and should look away.

In one workshop, a woman I'll call Laura was telling us how powerless she feels when it comes to money. Because her husband is the sole breadwinner, she is always on the receiving end when it comes to money, and she finds it hard to speak up when money decisions are being made. As she was talking about her sense of impotence, her posture literally began to slump. Her shoulders rounded, and we could hear her voice start to strain. It was like watching the money monster take over her body.

I've seen employees who normally speak in a steady voice talk a mile a minute and have trouble catching their breath when they come in to ask for a raise. I've seen others whose jaws get so tight they almost can't speak at all. They all might as well hang out a sign: Money Monsters at Work.

Look around you—in the office, among your friends, in interactions with business partners or customers or suppliers. Listen for changes in the pitch of the voice and the speed of talking when the conversation turns to money. Watch the person's posture and gestures. Whose breath quickens as she dives right into the conversation? And whose breath quickens because he wants to avoid the subject?

In all these cases, the physical manifestation is a signal that the person is on the verge of money madness behavior. Be forewarned. Pause. Watch where you step.

Tame the Monster

Think about it: Your adult money behavior is governed by emotions planted in you when you were a small child, before you had any understanding at all of money or how it works or what it can and cannot do for your life. What you thought of as your objective, grown-up money life is actually a bunch of immature, subjective responses dictated to you by your money monster.

And here's the heart of the matter: You can't fight the monster; you have to tame it. Fighting it only gives it more life.

Laura, the woman in our workshop who felt so powerless when it came to money, offers a good example. Her childhood money message—a not uncommon one—was that money equals self-worth, and you thus count a person's value by counting his dollars. Every time Laura shopped at the supermarket or made out the check to the utility company or distributed the kids' allowance, her money monster would remind her that she herself, having little money, had little value.

So sometimes, Laura would strike back. How? By going on a shopping spree. She'd head to the mall, credit card in hand, and shop her way through the clothing shop, the shoe store, the up-market home goods boutique, and the pamper-yourself bath and body products emporium. Maybe in just the moment that she piled up the packages in the cargo area of the car, she might have felt a flash of satisfying self-esteem. But only for that moment.

In spending money she didn't have, Laura had actually fed the money monster, given it even more power over her. After all, now she would have to go begging to her husband for more money to pay for the things she had bought—and she would thus accentuate again her own low worth.

It's like trying to sink a beach ball. You try pushing it down below the surface of the water, but it just keeps popping back up. The only way to sink a beach ball is to let the air out of it, and the only way to beat the money monster is to tame it. You'll never beat it down.

But to deflate the monster, it helps to be aware also of the consequences of your money madness behavior. So in the next step of this awareness cure, we'll calculate the costs of money madness.

Counting the Consequences and Calculating the Costs

An example of the effects of money madness may prove instructive. Mine. Because when it comes to the costly consequences of money madness, my experience was for me about as pricey as you can get.

Back in 1984, when I was just starting my career in finance, my stockbroker clued me in on a pair of aggressive and highly speculative start-up ventures—two companies that were developing innovative products and targeting specific niche markets. "A hundred bucks for every dollar you invest is not too much to hope for," the broker predicted. Even if she were exaggerating, I figured I would *at least* double my money.

I was in. I cleaned out my entire cash reserve of $10,000 and handed it over. Was I aware of the risks? Of course. You can't read the business press, much less get through Wharton Business School, without being treated to the cold, hard realities of entrepreneurship. One of those realities is that start-ups generally underperform at best and that very few survive, so my rational mind understood with perfect clarity that the odds were stacked against me.

But my rational mind was not in charge. My money madness was, and all I saw was a chance to get a lot of money—which to me of course was everything—for no effort at all. Something for nothing—or at least for very little: It's everybody's dream. I fell for it when I was seven years old and my friend and I decided we would each shoplift a toy from the stationery store, and I found it equally electrifying now.

The start-ups were duly launched, igniting my fantasies about the enormous payoff to come, while also sparking a lot of high-stress worry about all the things that could go wrong. In the end, just about everything went wrong. Both companies went belly-up, and my investment simply evaporated.

Did I lose the 10,000 bucks? You bet I did. But that was only the beginning. I really lost a great deal more.

How I Turned a $10,000 Loss into a $150,000+ Loss—It Was Easy!

I'll let you in on the dirty little secret about the money business: It doesn't take that much brains, talent, or effort to succeed at it.

This is one of the things that distinguishes the pursuit of money from other endeavors in life. Whether it's driving big rigs across the country, or heart surgery, or dog grooming, or particle physics, or playing rhythm section in a rock band, no one is going to hire you unless you can demonstrate that you know what you're doing and have the license or certificate to prove it.

But you can succeed in the world of money without having any particular aptitude, without any particular training or knowledge, without any particular skill. Where money is concerned, in fact, you can do the simple thing—the easy, effortless thing—and succeed.

Had I not been in the grip of my money madness in 1984, I very well might have done the simple thing and invested my savings, as millions of people do, in an ordinary mutual fund—for example, one pegged to the Standard & Poor's index of 500 stocks. Standard & Poor's (S&P), as I'll bet many of you know, is the nation's foremost rating agency when it comes to a stock's creditworthiness; investors look to these ratings as they consider various investment alternatives. The legendary S&P 500 index consists of 500 large, publicly held U.S. companies whose stocks are traded on Wall Street's two biggest stock markets: the New York Stock Exchange (NYSE) and the Nasdaq. It is considered the benchmark of how U.S. equities perform, and along with the Dow Jones Industrial Average, an index of 30 stocks traded on the NYSE, it is looked to as a bellwether of the economy. For that reason, many commercially marketed index funds mirror the S&P 500, holding the same 500 stocks in the same proportions as a way of trying to mimic similar performance.

History shows quite clearly that had I invested my $10,000 in a mutual fund mirroring the S&P 500 index in 1984, it would have grown to $154,548 over the 22-year period ending in 2006. Instead, my money monster drove me to try to knock a grand slam out of the park for instant success; I went for the high-stakes triumph—and lost it all.

I Lost Other Opportunities

As if $154,000 and change weren't a high enough price to pay for money madness, I also lost myriad other opportunities when I sank my 10 thou into that high-flying investment.

In 1990, for example, I was looking to buy a house. I sure could have used that lost $10,000 toward my down payment, and a bigger down payment would have made a big difference in the kind of house I was able to look for and eventually buy. Invested in an S&P 500 index fund in 1984, my original $10,000 would have grown to $28,118 by 1990. That would have made a *very* big difference in the kind of house I was able to buy.

A couple of years later, in 1992, I was expanding my business, taking on a partner, and was in the middle of negotiating the partnership arrangement. It was a stressful time; the business had been going through some growing pains, and my money monster was busy night and day filling me with the usual fears about security and survival. It meant I went into the partnership negotiations focused almost exclusively on the money I could get out of the deal.

Chances are I wouldn't have had so narrow a focus in 1992 if my bank account had included the $35,000+ that an S&P mutual fund would have earned on my original $10,000. That $35,000 might well have helped me approach the negotiations with less stress and a more flexible mind, one open to options and suggestions—instead of a mind fixated on my own security. Nervous about business, focused solely on cash, I made a deal that gave away a bit too much on the upside; it wasn't nearly as good as it could have been and should have been.

See what I mean? The money I lost was only the beginning. Add to it the money I didn't earn because I had lost the $10K. Then mix in the opportunities I missed, the narrowing of options, the open doors I was too blinded by money madness to see. It's a heavy price to pay.

Just Exactly How Much Does It Cost?

Rick and Joanne Randolph are the last people you'd think would forgo the inspection on a house they wanted to buy. They run a successful contracting business and are as sophisticated as people can be about the housing market and home-buying transactions. Or so everyone always assumed—until Rick and Joanne fell madly in love with the house of their dreams. Then all bets were off, and the pair managed to sweep under the rug or turn a blind eye to any obstacle to the purchase of the house.

The first and seemingly most compelling obstacle arose when the Randolphs failed to qualify for a mortgage. It turns out that although their business reaped a substantial income, they were also major spenders, and they just didn't have the down payment. The bank's rejection of their application was a blow, but it was also a chance to pull out of the contract. And had Rick and Joanne not been in the throes of money madness, that is almost surely what they would have done.

"A house is a great investment," they told themselves. "Isn't that what everyone says? If you rent, you're just throwing money down the drain, but if we buy this house, even if we have to struggle to make the payments for a while, it's an investment that will just keep increasing in value."

The hillside location of the house was highly desirable, the view of the lake was spectacular, the interior was beautifully designed, and Rick and Joanne did not want to think of themselves as people who couldn't afford the house. So they scrambled and scraped and borrowed and put down $150,000 in cash, agreed to a subprime mortgage, decided to skip the house inspection, and moved in.

Mistake upon mistake. It turned out that there were major problems with the electrical wiring and the plumbing in the house. These were things Rick might normally have attended to, but he was too busy working for clients so he and Joanne could afford the monthly payments. The contracting business is always iffy, but even in the best of times, there's only so much business you can do. It wasn't enough. The truth is it was never going to be enough.

The bank foreclosed on the house, but that wasn't all Rick and Joanne lost. They had mortgaged much more than the house they wanted to buy; they had also mortgaged their future financial prospects, the good name of their business, even their family life. Those things eroded piece by piece and were badly depleted by the time the bank foreclosure was sealed—all because the Randolphs were ruled by their money madness. Their minds were 90 percent focused on a fantasy each nurtured in the other and only 10 percent focused on the reality of numbers. Like co-conspirators or mutual enablers, they ignored each other's money madness, feeding each other's money delusions; where there should have been reciprocal checks on behavior, there were none.

Just take a look at the total bill Rick and Joanne are still paying after being seduced by the dream of home ownership, as rich a fantasy as my dream of earning 100 bucks for every dollar I invested in the two start-up companies:

Cost of the Randolphs' Money Madness

Item	Cost
Down payment—lost due to real estate downturn plus foreclosure and legal fees	$150,000
Credit rating	Ruined
Public relations impact on contracting business	Devastating
Financial stability and future prospects for contracting business	Questionable

Item	Cost
Marriage	Strained
Children	Stressed
Life/health	Adversely altered

What's the Cost of Lost Opportunities?

There's another way of looking at the cost of money madness, and that's to calculate how much you might have if you were free of the madness. Take the case of Alan and Sue Borden. Their joint annual income is substantial: Alan is the administrator of a hospital that is fast becoming the region's major medical center, and Sue is the principal in a boutique accounting firm that numbers among its clients the most thriving businesses in their growing prairie community. Yet the Bordens never quite make ends meet. They share with millions of their fellow consumers what I've called Prisoner of Spending behavior: the idea that they deserve whatever they can afford, and that they can afford whatever they can pay for, one way or the other.

The result is that they are always on a bill-paying treadmill and are virtually always tapped out. Each month, Alan chooses certain bills to "defer," knowing that late fees must be paid on the deferrals and worrying that the fees are getting higher. The Bordens shuffle their credit cards like a poker hand, trying to remember which cards are close to being maxed out so they can use one that isn't. It's tiring, and it's stressful.

They don't spend for ostentation, but with three kids and two adult professionals in the house, expenses mount, and the Bordens can rationalize every single one of them:

- They need the three vehicles in the driveway; both Bordens drive to work, and they use the pickup truck to haul stuff.
- They need a new laptop for every member of the family every three years. Alan and Sue both have to be wired

to their work, and kids today can't get through school without their own computer.

 ◆ They need the yearly upgrade to new skis with the latest in technological advances—plus accompanying gear and fashions. After all, skiing is their passion; it's the one activity they do as a family; good gear is not a luxury, it's a matter of safety.

The incessant noise of their consumer society tells them they need all this, and their money monster assures them they deserve it. Of course they do. Who doesn't? And, as the money monster reminds them, they can obviously afford it. After all, aren't they paying for it now?

Yes, and they're also paying all those late fees averaging $40 or so per month per unpaid bill, interest rates of at least 18 percent on their credit cards, and an incalculable amount in the constant anxiety both Sue and Alan wear like albatrosses around the neck.

The thing that keeps Sue up at night is that they have no reserve—no back-up savings to cushion a blow, should one befall them. People do get fired, after all—even highly placed administrators in prominent institutions. What would they do in an economic downturn if one or both of them were suddenly out of work? It doesn't bear thinking about.

So they don't think about it.

But what if they weren't paying all that they're now paying in late fees, high interest rates, and anxiety? What if they simply bought less, saving some of the money they now spend on all those things they deserve and can afford?

Suppose the Bordens had just two cars and no truck. Suppose the family shared a home desktop computer and Alan and Sue left their work at the office instead of being on call every minute of the day through their laptops. And suppose the five of them upgraded to new skis every three years. What would those changes mean in financial terms—and what might the financial difference mean to the Bordens' life and to Sue's night sleep?

See "The Bordens' Savings" for a reckoning of what they might have if they make those changes this year:

The Bordens' Savings

Item	Unit Cost	This Year's Savings
Truck (they can haul things in the two cars)	Truck payment: $260/month	$3,120
	Maintenance: $400/year	$400
Laptops	$1,500 per Borden	$7,500 less $1,000 for fully loaded desktop: $6,500
Skis with bindings	$750 per Borden	$3,750
Boots	$400 per Borden	$2,000
Ski pants	$70 per Borden	$350
Ski parka	$150 per Borden	$750
Total		$16,870

This year's total savings might make it easier to pay some bills on time, which would calm some of the stress Alan feels every month. But think what it might mean over 6 years, or 12, to be free of the money madness that keeps the Bordens buying and spending and keeping up with the latest in consumer offerings. Suppose they managed this year's savings for 6 years and ended up saving approximately $48,000—although with older skis than they might like. What would it mean to the Bordens' lives if they had that money back? What about the $96,000 over 12 years?

Like the road not taken, money not spent opens up other possibilities. It makes us available for options we cannot know about in advance. For the Bordens, it would mean a reserve cushion that would let them sleep at night.

Lost opportunities and lost sleep. The question has to be asked: What is your money madness costing you? It's time to compute the price tag.

What Your Money Madness Is Costing You

This exercise asks you to think of four madness-driven mistakes in your life—one in each of the key categories of earning, spending, saving, and investing—so we can tally the cost of the mistakes. Of course, there may be categories in which you have not been driven to make mistakes, and there may be categories in which you have made multiple mistakes.

What do I mean by *mistakes*? I don't mean those expenditures, even very pricey expenditures, that have paid you back over and over or may do so in the future—like the premier speaker system that gives you endless hours of untold pleasure, or your house, which carries a rich monthly cost but which you'll sell one day to fund your retirement. Spending or investing money you can afford in ways that enrich your life is not money madness.

What I'm talking about are the money life events you wish you could undo because they took something away from your life.

For an earning mistake, think of my friend Jack and the money madness that makes it impossible for him to ask for a raise. The cost? In financial terms alone, the discrepancy between what Jack should have been paid and what he has settled for is substantial.

Or what about the hot tub my neighbor Gary thought he had to have to recapture his youth, but that now sits empty on his deck, its canvas cover mildewing by the minute? You know what hot tubs cost these days—and how hard it is to sell or even give away used ones? That's a pricey spending mistake.

I have a client I'll call Catherine who has persistently rejected all advice to start a monthly savings plan because she claims she needs every penny to pay her bills. The cost? In a sudden emergency, Cathy had no reserve to fall back on—and instead had to go into debt to keep her life and family afloat.

This book has already recounted numerous investing mistakes—like Bill putting all his money on a single tech stock, only to lose just about everything, or my own colossally foolish $10,000 investment in my 20s, the costs of which you saw calculated a couple of pages ago.

But that's not the whole picture. The one cost I did not share with you—a cost you'll also compute for your madness-driven mistakes—is the amount of money I would have made over my *lifetime* if I hadn't made the mistake in the first place. If I were madness-free and had put that $10,000 into a diversified portfolio instead of into the two start-ups, want to know how much I would have realized over my expected lifetime? By age 90, which is more or less what the insurance actuaries compute to be my life span, I would have a check for approximately $20 million, which is equivalent to $5.5 million in today's purchasing power. That is what my hapless $10,000 could have been worth if I hadn't blown it through money madness.

When you do a similar calculation, you'll see in clear, uncomplicated numbers just exactly how much your money madness is costing you.

Start by confessing your mistakes. Now calculate what they cost. For Jack, the dollar cost is the difference between what his talent and experience would make him worth on the job market and his actual current compensation. For Gary, it's the cost of the hot tub—and maybe the cost of getting rid of the hot tub. For Catherine, it's the debt she'll need to repay—with interest. Put a dollar figure to your mistakes.

As to the nonfinancial costs of the mistakes, only you yourself can judge those.

Now add up the dollar costs for each category in which you've confessed mistakes: earning, investing, spending, saving. Then divide each category's total by the number of years of your adulthood to arrive at a per-year financial cost for the category. We'll assume that adulthood starts at 21, so count up the number of years you are older than 21, and that is the number to use. For example, if you're 34, you would divide each category total by 13 (34−21) to get the cost per year.

What My Money Madness Costs Me			
Category	My Madness-Driven Mistake	What It Cost	Cost Per Year*
Earning			
Earning Total Cost			
Investing			
Investing Total Cost			
Spending			
Spending Total Cost			
Savings			
Savings Total Cost			
Annual cost of my money madness			

*Divide "what it cost" by your age minus 21.

Add up the figures in the last column. That's the annual cost of your money madness.

Now let's take it a step further and calculate what these madness-driven mistakes are costing you over a lifetime—that is, what money are you not accruing because your money madness drives your money behavior?

You'll need to refer to the "If I Were Madness-Free" chart to do this calculation. It contains a multiplier for calculating the present value of your money madness bill compounded over what's left of your life, assuming an average life span of 90 years. We're also assuming a 10 percent a year growth on investments; that's lower than what has typically been achieved by the S&P index—and it is significantly lower than what has been achieved with my Rainbow Portfolio, as we'll see later.

Step 1: Take the annual cost of your money madness mistakes you calculated earlier.

Step 2: Find your appropriate age—or the closest equivalent—in the left-hand column of the "If I Were Madness-Free" chart.

Step 3: Multiply your per-year money madness bill by the multiplier number in the right-hand column.

If I Were Madness-Free

Your Age	Multiplier
25	788
30	567
35	407
40	292
45	209
50	150
55	106
60	75
65	52
70	35
75	23
80	14
85	7

The resulting number is the potential financial payoff you can look forward to if you can stop being ruled by the money monster of your emotions.

Here's the formula in a nutshell:

Total annual cost of your money madness x Your multiplier =
Cost of your money madness

A Cost of Money Madness Gallery

Let's say you're 40. Over the years, your money madness has driven you to make some stupendous mistakes: the wrong house, the wrong divorce settlement, the wrong job move, several wrong business decisions, a failure to save, and more. You've added them up category by category, and the total cost of all these mistakes comes to $133,000. At 40, you're 19 years older than 21, so divide the total by 19 to get the yearly cost of your money madness—in this case, $7,000 a year.

Now, take that $7,000 and multiply it by the multiplier for your age, 292. The bottom line is $2 million plus, which represents the amount of money—in today's dollars—that you will have at age 90 if you cure your money madness today and invest the money in a boring S&P portfolio instead.

Let's take another example. Say you're 25 years old and you figured the yearly cost of your money madness, in just the few short years you've been working, at a cool $5,000 per year. Flush with the excitement of a good job with a good paycheck, you've given your money monster free rein. There was the high-priced membership at the gym you never go to, the top-of-the-line high-tech refrigerator that only ever holds a six-pack of beer, and the vintage Mercedes that spends more time in the shop than on the road. There were also a few foolish investments—thanks to those tips from your friend with an "in" to Wall Street—not to mention the wrong guess on interest rates when you took out that adjustable rate mortgage. And when you tote it all up, you're surprised to see that it's costing you that much. You ain't seen nothing yet, for when you take that $5,000 in yearly madness cost and multiply it by the multiplier for your age, 788, it comes out to $3.9 million. That's what you can gain over your lifetime if you stop being ruled by the money monster of your emotions.

Any way you figure it, however, your money madness is costing you a lot of money, not to mention all the other things it is costing you. But just look at the size of the financial opportunity—the cold, hard cash you could have—if you were madness-free.

And money is just the beginning.

Freedom from Money Madness Means More Than More Money

The flip side of the high cost of money madness is the high payoff of being madness-free. We've just seen exactly how big that payoff can be in sheer dollars. In my case, curing myself of my money madness had the effect of turning me into a virtual money magnet. Precisely because I was no longer striving after money in that desperate way, money flowed to me readily. Clients saw a confident, comfortable man—and were suddenly eager to pay for that man's services. Prospective clients met with a professional who wanted a partnership that would be mutually beneficial, and they were suddenly eager to sign up. But all this was just the start of the cure's payoff.

Just about everything else changed as well. Not stopping in my tracks and racing for the nearest stock ticker whenever I overhear the word "market" has altered my life considerably. I don't wake up these days in a panic to check out what the Nikkei and the Hang Seng did overnight. Needless to say, that has made me a calmer man.

Without the stress of money madness, I'm also a healthier man, despite being 20 years older. Now that my life is no longer the thing that's "happening while I'm making other plans," in the immortal words of John Lennon, I have time to hike and bike and stretch mentally as well as physically. The health rewards have been unexpected.

The same could happen to you, and it makes sense to consider how. If your personal money monster no longer had you by the throat and you were madness-free, what would be the payoff? Let's look at it in every aspect of your life.

Imagine the Payoff in Investing

If you're the way I was and can't resist a hot stock tip, you probably can't wait for the end of this chapter so you can check the Web or the cable networks for the latest market update. Maybe your latest hot stock is going up, and maybe it's tanking, but the point is you're there watching every uptick and downturn—and holding your breath through it all. Or maybe your money madness is just the opposite: You refuse to pay attention to your portfolio; that's your broker's job, and you don't want to know. Either way, you're not getting as good a return on your investment as you could—which means you'll reach financial independence at 70 instead of at 60, either stressed out or numbed out by the whole issue of investments. Think of the payoff if you were free of this madness. Write it down:

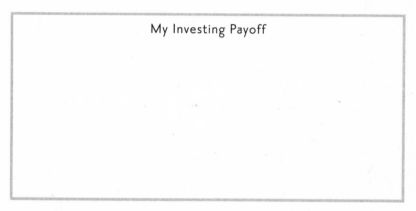

My Investing Payoff

Imagine the Payoff for Spending, Giving, and Saving

In spending, giving, and saving, chances are your money monster has you going one of two ways. Either you're overspending—to buy happiness or love or both—and undersaving. Or you're underspending because money is security, and therefore you're saving too much. If you're the overspending type, you're probably not going to have enough for your children's college education, your trip of a lifetime, that second home you've always wanted, or health care, which you'll need at the end of a long, long work life. If you underspend, you're so future-oriented you may die before you get a chance to enjoy the money you keep squirreling away. In either case, imagine the payoff if you were free of this madness. Imagine a life lived today, in sync with your heartbeat, without striving or pressure or fear of the future. Think about spending, giving, and saving in accord with your values, not to impress others or reach some inherited goal.

My Spending Payoff

My Giving Payoff

My Saving Payoff

Imagine the Payoff at Work

Think about going to work or running your business without that money monster hissing in your ear telling you how to behave. If you no longer measure your self-worth in terms of what you earn in a day or a year, think how you might express your true value. You won't have to spend all your energy stressing over your fee, leaving you few resources to do the job. You won't have to fear scarcity or isolate yourself from your co-workers; instead, you'll be open to opportunity and to cooperating to exploit it. The result can be real riches—financial and otherwise.

My Work or Business Payoff

Imagine the Payoff at Home

Your home is both where you live and how you live. Think about the payoff if your home offered total comfort both actually and metaphorically—with no more closed doors between you and the people who share your home.

Imagine the payoff if you could look at your house not as something that makes a statement about you but as a place to live—comfortably, including in financial comfort.

My Home Payoff

Imagine if money were no longer the last closed door between you and your spouse or partner or in a friendship or family relationship. Think about the closeness that can bring, and imagine it for your own relationships.

My Relationship Payoff

It sounds enriching, doesn't it? And you're getting there. In the next step of the awareness cure, you'll use what you've learned about your own money madness, its consequences, and its costs to bring your own money monster to heel.

CHAPTER 4

Free Your Life from Money Madness

Tame the Monster

Take a deep breath. Inhale through the nose and let your belly, rib cage, and chest expand as you fill your lungs with air. One, two, three seconds.

At the top of the inhalation, lungs filled, pause for one second.

Now exhale, letting your breath out easily through your open mouth for six seconds—twice as long as your inhale. Five, six, seven, eight, nine, ten.

At the bottom of the exhale, say to yourself, aloud if you can: "May my money wisdom increase."

I call it the Money Breath. It combines a little Eastern wisdom, a little Western exercise physiology, and a large dollop of the cure for money madness. Its aim is to break your money madness pattern, interrupt the automatic response, and create a gap in your thinking that wisdom can fill. I do the Money Breath whenever I'm involved in just about any money transaction, whether it's rebalancing my investment portfolio, shopping at my local bookstore, paying for our recent kitchen renovation, or buying new clothes for the kids. About the only time I don't do the Money Breath is when I get myself a half-dozen mangoes, my favorite fruit.

By now, in fact, doing the Money Breath is automatic for me. For years, however, I did it consciously and deliberately. I had to remind myself to do it every time.

I recommend you do the same. Practice the Money Breath assiduously—even when you're buying your morning paper. As you reach for your wallet or pick up the phone to call your broker or head into your annual performance review with the boss, just stop. Come to a standstill, take 10 seconds, do the Money Breath, and ask for money wisdom.

The Money Breath: The Pause That Refreshes

The Money Breath is a simple tool for fighting money madness. It has a curative power that is both physiological and mental.

Physiologically, any time an emotion like the one that drives your money monster is triggered—whether it's fear, anxiety, greed, resignation, envy, ambition, the need to win, whatever—it causes an adrenaline rush in the body. That, in turn, constricts your blood flow, speeding up your breathing and making it more shallow. Shallow breathing means that less oxygen gets to the brain; less oxygen to the brain means the brain doesn't work as well as it can or should.

Doing the Money Breath burns off the excess adrenaline your money monster has prompted. It relaxes the blood flow and deepens your breathing so that more oxygen gets to the brain. You think more clearly. Clearly enough to note to yourself that it's your money monster telling you that you deserve the new car or need to invest in CNBC's latest stock pick or probably shouldn't ask for a raise this year. In fact, the money monster flourishes in a short-of-breath, anaerobic environment. Do the money breath, and you flood the environment with oxygen, making it inhospitable to the money monster.

But the change is also mental and emotional. In the 10 seconds of the money breath, **you slow everything down enough to be able to question your reflexive responses to your money monster; the little mantra at the end is a gentle reminder to invite your adult wisdom in to confront your childhood money message.**

That's what this chapter is about: using the awareness of your money madness that you've gained in the previous chapters to begin to cure the madness.

This chapter presents three exercises, in addition to the Money Breath, that can empower you to confront your childhood money message whenever money is an issue. The first helps you disarm your money monster. The second helps you challenge your money behavior by changing the context. The third shows you how to break the pattern of your behavior.

There's a logic to the sequence: emotion, mind, action—feel, understand, do. First, you accept—even embrace—your money monster and the feelings the monster brings without fighting him. Then you change the context and shift your mind-set. Finally, you break the pattern by changing your conduct.

You may want to set aside some time and space to do these three exercises. But start doing the Money Breath now. Today. Think about a money challenge, and do the breath this second. Keep at it. In time, it will keep you from being ruled by your money monster.

Right now, however, start by shaking hands with him.

Exercise I
Shake Hands with Your Money Monster

Do you know the saying that you can't rewrite the past? You're about to confound the saying and do just that—rewrite your own past.

In Chapter 3, you recalled being initiated into the money world. In this exercise, you're going to delve more deeply into that recollection.

Maybe your initiation was the day you got your first allowance. Maybe it came from overhearing your parents arguing about money. Or perhaps you visited a friend whose house was so much bigger and grander—or smaller and shabbier—than yours.

Whatever the nature of the initiation, it made you aware of money—how it was spent, saved, invested, discussed, fretted over—as a force in the life of your family. You saw its impact, how it affected your parents' relationship with one another, how it fit into your family's relationship with the world, how it colored your own life.

Describe the initiation in writing—only instead of using the pronoun I to tell the story, write it in the third person. Give yourself another name—preferably a name without any personal associations at all—and write the story about that person.

You'll see it differently. By telling the story about "someone else," you'll achieve a certain distance from the event. Distance, however, can't defuse the feelings the money initiation stirred, feelings that no doubt come flooding back as you write, the same feelings that surface in you today whenever you're in a money situation. Note them in the margins. By looking at them as if they were happening to someone else, you can actually see them more clearly, objectively, and in their true proportion.

That's what happened to me. I wrote down the story about a boy I called Adam asking his father one night in the kitchen how much money he made. I wrote about Adam's father becoming enraged at the question and about the way he stared at his son. I could see and feel Adam's shame and fear, and I understood immediately how he concluded, consciously or unconsciously, that he would do anything to avoid seeing his father angry like that again; he would do anything to avoid feeling the shame and fear that paternal anger stirred in him. It was easy to understand how that quickly translated for Adam into earning and holding on to as much money as he could.

For what this third-person rewrite of the past really shows us is how our adult money behavior is a way of running from childhood pain. **The running, however, simply emboldens the money monster— in the same way that fleeing a mountain lion just triggers its instinct to chase.**

That is why the thing to do next, once you have written the story and cataloged the emotions it triggers, is to change the ending. Instead of running from the pain—which is instinctive and offers an instant if short-term advantage—think about what else you might have done. Your assignment is to come up with three other possible ways you could have responded to the event.

For example, I eventually realized that instead of shame and fear, Adam could have felt compassion for his father, sadness for the way he equated financial worth with self-worth, and sympathy for his desire not to burden Adam with adult matters. Adam could have asked his father openly: "Is money something to be afraid of?" Maybe Adam's father really wanted to protect his young son from too great a concern over money at such a young age. Maybe his response was really an expression of love.

Once I saw the alternate endings of Adam's story, I realized that all my anxiety around money came from the story *I had made up in re-*

sponse to that moment of shame and fear in my childhood. The story I had contrived had been about security and money, and now I saw, writing in the third person, that the story in fact could have been about something else. Once I saw that, I was no longer the pawn of the money-is-everything script, and I didn't have to run from the shame and fear anymore. Instead, I could allow myself to just stand there and be enveloped by the feelings—without trying to avoid or change them. The stillness alone was a remarkably powerful weapon against my money monster's power. For it turns out that the monster will attack only if he's armed with the right story; when you change the story, he's powerless.

It's a little like finding yourself in the presence of a bee buzzing closer and closer around you. The bee is almost surely getting ready to sting you—for good reason: You are a predator, and it must protect its colony. What do you do? You can duck and bob and weave, but you can't escape; bees have been known to chase people the length of a football field and more. You can flail your arms around or pick up the nearest Louisville Slugger and try to swat the bee out of the park, but all that does is exacerbate the bee's stinging impulse. You can't bat a bee. No, your best bet is just to stand there; your very stillness is your best protection.

Retelling my own story from the distance of a third-person vantage point let me see more clearly the eight-year-old feelings that drove my money life. And coming up with alternate endings made me realize that all the racing around and bee-chasing of my money life were just that—childhood feelings ruling my adult behavior. It made it possible for me to just stand there, just hang out with the feelings—and not get stung.

Once this exercise has planted this realization in your brain, it will take root there. And each time your money monster rises up inside you—and he will continue to do so indefinitely—you will find yourself less and less in his thrall. "There he goes again," you'll hear yourself thinking; "it's just my money monster. I don't have to do anything except just stand there beside him, or maybe even invite him in."

Shake Hands with Your Money Monster:
Summary

1. Recall a key money initiation event of your childhood.
2. Write a description of the event, referring to yourself in the third person.
3. Come up with three alternate endings to the story.

Exercise 2
Change the Context, Challenge the Behavior

You wouldn't ride your bicycle into the Metropolitan Opera House during a performance. You wouldn't take your horse to the office. You wouldn't hang your laundry up to dry in the aisle of the supermarket. All those behaviors would be inappropriate to the context, and we humans are highly attuned to context. In fact, it influences just about all aspects of our behavior.

So the context of the Met Opera, for example—the kind of place it is, what happens there, the other people in attendance—would prompt you to act in some very specific ways. You would dress with a certain formality. You would stop talking once the lights went down. At the end of the performance, you would politely at least, enthusiastically at best, applaud the singers and instrumentalists. The context, in short, would dictate the norms of your behavior. That's the way the world and human psychology work.

And as psychologists tell us, if you change the context, you have a good chance of challenging one pattern of behavior and making it yield to another pattern of behavior, one that is appropriate to the new, changed context.

This exercise asks you to change the context of your money life *in your mind*—to create a new way of behaving around money in fantasy only, on the theory that just making the mental breakthrough can shift your energy and spur you to challenge your usual pattern of behavior. You'll change the context twice:

First, fantasize that your money just doubled. Your income from every source—job, rental property, stock dividends, whatever—is twice what it currently is, and all your assets—house, investments, and so on—have just doubled in value.

What would change? How would your life expand? How would you spend your time differently? Would you quit your job? Buy a Porsche or a Prius? Take off with the love of your life for an extended vacation? Write down the changes you would make and the ways in which you imagine that your life would blossom if you had twice as much money as you have today.

Second, imagine the opposite. A historic global recession has set in, and starting right now, all of your income and the value of all of your assets have gone down by 50 percent. What changes now? How will you continue to live as richly as you're living today? Figure it out.

The idea of this exercise is simply to show you how a different context gives rise to different behavior. That should be a window into your money life—and into your routine acceptance of your money madness. In other words, the behavior that your money madness dictates isn't the sole and exclusive behavior you can have. It isn't a formula carved in stone from which you may not deviate. You may deviate from it any which way; if you had to, as this exercise shows, you would.

When Anne and I assign this exercise in workshops, we find it invariably brings smiles to the faces of workshop participants. No one has ever been stumped by either of these questions. In fact, both the expansion and the diminution of money resources seem to prompt people to become more creative. In both instances, they're able to cut to the bone of what's valuable in their lives—and that is liberating.

Try it. See if the new contexts don't move your mind-set a position or two off the base of money madness it's been sitting on all these years. That, in turn, should rotate your behavior ever so slightly. It's a beginning.

Change the Context, Challenge the Behavior: Summary

1. Imagine first that you have twice the money you have today. How will that change the way you live your life?
2. Imagine next that you have half your current financial

---

assets and income. How will that change the way you live your life?

3. What do the changes you've noted tell you about your current money behavior?

Exercise 3
Break the Pattern

A good way to stop doing what you habitually do is to make yourself do the opposite. This exercise offers practice in just such a role reversal when it comes to your money behavior.

What's the most noticeable aspect of your money behavior? Whatever it is, do the exact opposite—for one full week.

If you're a saver, start spending. If you're a spender, start saving. If, as I used to, you constantly check the markets online, scan every stock ticker you see, and turn up the radio for news about overseas exchanges, force yourself to blot all that out of your life. Delete the market report from your home page, close your eyes when the stock ticker crawls across the bottom of the TV screen, turn off the radio when the business news comes on.

If you're an impulse buyer, head for the mall with no credit cards and only enough cash for parking. Now walk past all your favorite shops, browse, window shop, and head for home.

Note the feelings that come up as you reverse your role, and mine those feelings for insights into your money madness.

Have fun reversing roles. If you're a saver who is not used to spending, make a plan to spend a certain amount each day of the week or to spend in a different store each day of the week or to buy something for yourself and something for someone you love on alternate days. How does it feel?

If you're a spender determined to save, make a ritual of it. You can start small and with spare change by getting hold of seven shoe boxes, one for each day of the week, and labeling each with a different saving purpose, for example: "Dinner Out," "Car Speakers," "Dream Vacation," "Christmas Gifts," "Digital Camera," "Road Trip," "College Fund." From the amount you generally allocate for entertainment, for example, apportion a certain amount for Dinner Out, a certain amount for Car Speakers, and a certain amount for Digital Camera. Because each will get a hit of savings once a week, divide each apportioned amount by 50—not 52, as we'll assume two weeks off for vacation when the shoe boxes won't be around—and that's your weekly shoe box contribution. For example, if you have apportioned $1,000 for Dinner Out for the year, your weekly contribution to that shoe box would be $20 ($1,000 ÷ 50).

The son of a shoe salesman, I did this exercise years ago and found that the tactile immediacy of the shoe boxes—which were easy for me to get hold of—made the exercise both fun and compelling. In fact, my wife and I recently started the shoe box system for our monthly clothing, dining out, and entertainment expenditures and find it works better than bank accounts—and is far more enjoyable.

Are you the archetypal conservative investor who hews to CDs and bank instruments? Try risking just a bit beyond your comfort: Invest a little money in equities. What does it feel like—and what does the feeling tell you about the fear that kept you from investing in equities all this time? Has the fear perhaps held you back from new, expansive life opportunities? Is there a way to risk safely—like a rock climber who is roped and belayed?

By contrast, if you're a risk-loving investor who likes to speculate, force yourself to buy a six-month CD at a rate of return you would normally spurn. Experience what it's like to exchange your usual adrenaline rush for the feeling that your money is fully insured and growing—slowly and perhaps minimally, but surely. Is it possible that the rush was really always the point? Could it be that there are other ways to get the rush than through money?

Keep it up: Undo a different pattern each week. As you do so, sift your feelings. Examine them. What are you learning? After all, the point of this role reversal exercise is to provoke yourself out of a rut, to make yourself uncomfortable, and thereby to produce an insight. The idea is to show the risk-loving investor that what she loves is the adrenaline rush. The point is to let the scared investor look his fear in the eye, see where it comes from, understand how it informs his behavior. The insight is what counts, for that's what will let you be at peace with your money life.

My insight? When I did this exercise and forced myself not to look at the market news, I found that I really wasn't driven by a passion for finance but rather by sheer boredom and a lot of anxiety. It wasn't the market itself that intrigued me; it was the adrenaline rush—the heady anticipation that preceded my finding out about the market. I wasn't upset for the reason I thought I was upset, and my money madness wasn't about money; it was about something deeper and more important—an emptiness I tried not to feel by striving after money instead.

Break the Pattern:
Summary

1. Define your pattern.
2. Do the opposite for one week.
3. Note your feelings. What are you learning about why you do what you do?

The Awareness Cure for Money Madness

Your money monster may still be in the room with you when you confront the boss and ask for the raise, whispering your childhood money message into your ear as always. But by now, you see the monster for what it is, and the childhood money message it repeats is just so much static.

You now have the power to be in charge. You can turn down the volume on the childhood money message. You can command your money monster to sit down and be quiet while you consider whether to invest in that stock you heard the guy on the train talk about, or accept the offer on your house, or make an offer on another house. You've proven to yourself that your behavior when it comes to money is really your choice.

Keep practicing it. And keep breathing. You'll need all the awareness you can muster as we turn in Chapter 5 to that area of life where money madness can wreak particular havoc—your relationship with someone you love, now or in the future. But even if you're not in a relationship now, even if you are never in a relationship, doing the exercises in Chapter 5 is still an essential part of the Cure for Money Madness.

CHAPTER 5

Financial Intimacy

Getting Naked Around Money

What is the best way to increase intimacy with your spouse or partner? The standard answer is to talk openly and freely about sex, plunge right into the details of lovemaking, discuss with your partner your deepest desires, and reveal your most closely held sexual secrets.

Well, that probably couldn't hurt. But if you really want to heighten the intensity of your relationship, deepen the love you have for one another, and enrich and enhance your sex life, the right answer is to talk about money.

Money?

Absolutely. Think about it. For the past 50 years or so, we've all been encouraged to be open and honest about our emotions. For at least the last 35 years, we've been assured that we'll feel better if we come clean to our spouse or partner about our sexual indiscretions, if any. The Dr. Ruths of this world have actually gotten us to open up about the very mechanics of sex—and to make our preferences known to our partners in exquisite detail. We're so busy talking to one another about our feelings, confessing our affairs, and finding just the right words to tell our partners exactly what we'd like to have happen in bed that we haven't bothered with that other dark corner in a relationship—money. Yet that's where the secrets are—and that's where the next incremental uptick in intimacy can be found.

How many couples do you know who tell the absolute truth to one another about all the money issues in their relationship? We all know spouses who shave big bucks off the price they admit to paying for something. I have a friend who has an unvoiced expectation that her husband will always support her comfortably, while he's afraid to reveal that his income keeps falling. Another has a credit card his wife knows nothing about—as he told me in private. What he doesn't know is that his wife told me, also in private, that she has a credit card *he* knows nothing about—even though she pays for it out of household money he thinks is buying cleaning supplies and his gym socks.

Secrecy. Cover-ups. Hiding places. Equivocation. In some cases, outright lies. Where is the trust in a relationship where such things take place? What happens to intimacy when trust is eroded? Put as bluntly as possible, if there are secrets in a relationship, the intimacy is diminished and the sex is flatlined.

I call it the wisdom of the body. Keep a corner of yourself hidden from your partner, and something in your sexuality simply shuts down. There's a wall there somewhere—a lack of trust forming a barrier—and it makes you hold back and close down so that you're not giving as fully or as passionately as you can. As you'd like to. Jung put it well when he said that "pathology comes from a story untold." And pathology and intimacy don't mix.

But shine a light on this dark corner of your relationship, tell the story, share the money secrets you've kept, throw off the disguises you've been hiding behind, and you'll remedy the pathology and ratchet up your intimacy in ways you cannot even imagine.

Just consider: If you can talk openly and freely about this subject that tends to distance you from your partner or spouse, this possibly frequent focus of your arguments with one another (even if as a surrogate for other issues), if you can peel away the layers of money madness from each of your lives—challenging as it might be, what might you discover about each other?

You might then reveal secrets, express needs, share vulnerabilities, relate fears, assert desires neither of you has previously known. **Money talk, therefore, becomes a whole new way to strengthen a couple's intimacy. It's the new foreplay.**

Sure, some of the prohibition against this type of talk is cultural. In India, for example, a nation whose religious traditions are far more open about sex than our Western religions—and with a rich history of erotic art—any discussion of sex at any time is considered totally inappropriate, even between spouses. Yet it is perfectly acceptable in India to discuss money till the sacred cows come home. What you paid for that shirt, how much you cleared on your latest deal, the amount you lost on the deal before that, your annual income, the price of your house: All are fair game for conversation and are openly discussed.

It's precisely the opposite in most Western cultures. A friend told me about being at a dinner party recently where a well-known author was in attendance. The conversation roamed easily over the latest findings about oral sex among teenagers and the erotic pleasures of vacationing without your children. But when someone had the nerve to ask the author the size of the advance for his latest book, an appalled silence descended over the assembled guests. The author was stunned, insulted, and outraged. Justifiably, said the other couples to one another as they headed home soon after the embarrassing *faux pas* had been skillfully offset by the hostess. After all, what happens between an individual and his money is highly personal, and in the land of the almighty dollar, it is considered downright rude to ask about it.

And certainly, power lurks behind the prohibition as well. Traditionally in a relationship—but of course not always—the man holds power over the money while the woman holds power over sex. I know that the reason that has been true is that sex has historically been the only realm in which women *could* exercise power, property and assets being denied to them by law and/or custom. But whatever the antecedent, the tradition is there. A wife might resent her husband's control of the purse strings and compensate for it by controlling their sex life. And vice versa: A man may resent his wife's power as gatekeeper of sexuality and retaliate by putting a lock on all money knowledge. Even when latent, the power equation is there: She can shut down the sex; he can close the door on the money.

But while sex has become something couples feel comfortable talking about freely, money remains taboo—the last taboo in a relationship and the final barrier to real intimacy, true partnership, and a more fulfilling sex life.

My Story

Back in Chapter 2, I confessed that when I first met the woman who would become my wife, I barely waited for our second date before I discoursed at ease, at length, and in detail about my dating past and my earlier relationships. Money, however, was an altogether different matter.

Money was my fortress, which no one else could enter. It held my deepest secrets and my deepest needs. I suppose my specific fear vis-à-vis this woman I was beginning to feel very strongly about was twofold: If she knew how much money I had, she might love my money, not me, and if she knew how much money I had, she might want to spend it—with abandon. So in a sense I was simultaneously afraid that money would keep her from me and that she would keep me from my money. Weird.

For her part, Janine never told me that for the eight years she had been working—and earning an excellent salary that was regularly raised—she had never yet managed to save anything and struggled to live within her means. This was perhaps not surprising given an upbringing in which money was simply not a comfortable topic of discussion, and where girls were not expected to know about numbers, dollars, and markets—topics considered the exclusive realm of the males of her family.

Neither of us shared these secrets with one another. We talked endlessly about absolutely everything else, but not about money. We knew one another's politics, held lengthy discussions about religion, had vetted each other's favorite movies, books, vacation destinations, and ethnic cuisines. But we had no idea about each other's views or values when it came to spending, giving, saving, investing, insurance, or our dreams of a financial future.

I don't think our story is unusual. From my experience as both a financial advisor to couples and as a leader of couples workshops, it's clear to me that most couples at the start of a relationship neglect the whole issue of money. They go along as we did during courtship, just assuming that such things would work themselves out somehow. I never asked Janine the details of her money life—perhaps as a way of preventing her from asking me the details of mine. And I certainly never offered any details, for as we know, a key component of my childhood money message was that money just isn't talked about. If a father and son didn't talk about it, neither did a husband and wife.

So Janine and I continued to maintain separate accounts as we got closer and closer to marriage. We each paid half the rent on the apartment we were now sharing. We split our household expenses, although not according to any logic or formula, and we each paid for our own clothing and incidentals. And when it came time for a big-ticket item like a vacation, it was just sort of assumed that I would take care of that—the male as gatekeeper of the money. We were in love, after all, and it wouldn't have been romantic to discuss money specifics.

Two Live More Expensively Than One Plus One

Once we were married, the pattern of vagueness continued, as I believe it does for most couples. Vagueness isn't possible when you're single; when you are the sole breadwinner in a household consisting of yourself, you can be absolutely positive that you're accountable for every penny. Not so once you marry or become half of a couple; instead, because neither knows exactly what the money situation is, it's easy for each partner to just assume that there's an abundance that will take care of any expenditure.

You figure there are two incomes now, so it's okay to pay the higher price or max out the credit card this month—forgetting that your spouse or partner may well be thinking the exact same thing. The new largesse of couplehood blinds you; you just don't feel that accountable any more.

Something else happens when two single people become a couple. You find out it isn't true that two can live as cheaply as one. In fact, what invariably happens is that the two of you begin to live at the level of the higher spender in each category of spending.

In our case, for example, my spending predilection had always been that when I ate out, I liked to do so at a high-priced restaurant noted for its fine chef. Janine, when she was single, couldn't have cared less about haute-cuisine restaurants, but she did have a penchant for buying any and every book that caught her fancy. Neither of us was about to give up these preferences once we were married: We dined out together at my favorite expensive eateries, then strolled to the nearest bookstore and both bought every title that looked interesting. Each of us, in short, rose to the higher level of spending in our separate categories of predilection. The two of us were now living more expensively than either of us had lived when single; and like most couples, we didn't even notice it happening.

In fact, we steadfastly refused to notice anything at all having to do with money. True, there was a new urgency to the burden of my money madness. Concealing from Janine the fact that my money behavior was governed by the responses of an eight-year-old not only seemed a little dishonest but also made me rather lonely. Every time I made an investment and didn't tell Janine about it felt like a weight on my shoulders. Every time I proposed something and she asked if we could afford it, I heard myself prevaricating and felt myself posturing—and I didn't like it.

For her part, as I would learn much later, the burden was equally weighty. She too felt lonely—excluded from money decisions she sensed were being made without her. Infantilized by the feeling that money was a subject she couldn't master. Guilty over the idea that she was spending "somebody else's" money.

There we were in the classic power split, each of us controlling what we had in our power to control, me calling the shots on money, Janine calling the shots on intimacy. But control is not good for relationships. Control separates people; you can't compel trust or blast your way to passion. Trust and passion come from giving up control. A year into our marriage, Janine and I seemed to be moving in the opposite direction from trust and passion, and we were both feeling our intimacy eroding.

Then we moved to California and went shopping for our first house, and there it all was on the mortgage application: income, assets, liabilities, the whole financial record in black and white for my wife to see for herself. My fortress was breached. My secret was out. At long last, I was financially naked in front of my wife.

It made me very, very uncomfortable. It also made me sigh with relief.

Your Financial Intimacy Quotient

Getting naked around money is as essential for both partners in a relationship as sharing your feelings. Put another way, financial intimacy is as important as emotional intimacy. In fact, they're really two sides of a coin.

What do I mean by the term *financial intimacy?* It comes from my initial meeting with Anne Watts. I had been a participant in a couples communication workshop Anne was leading and had found it a life-changing experience, as Anne's workshops typically are. We met for a talk afterward, and Anne, hearing I was a financial advisor, told me how often the issue of money emerged as an obstacle to her clients' attempts to create more loving, fulfilling relationships. Funny, I replied; as I work with couples to improve their cash flow and retirement planning, I more and more find that what they really need first is a sense of connection and closeness with one another—sufficient intimacy to share their values.

It was certainly ironic. I, the money guy, had come to see that the greatest obstacle to financial success is the emotionally twisted set of perceptions we carry with us from childhood. Anne, with 22 years of experience as a sex therapist and intimacy counselor, had concluded that where relationships are concerned, money is more momentous than sex. But the irony turned on a lightbulb in both our brains, illuminating a seemingly simple formula: Get clear on the money, and greater intimacy can result; improve the intimacy of your relationship, and more money will flow. It's the basis of the financial intimacy workshops we've been running jointly since 2000, and it was the launching pad for this book.

In every relationship, there's double everything. You have his 'n' hers towels, designated sides of the bed, and two versions of money madness—yours and your partner's. Two money histories. Two sets of childhood money messages. You're just beginning to recognize the existence of these things in your own life, and if your spouse or partner is reading this book with you, he or she is just now beginning to confront these issues as well. It's the perfect time to get it all out there, introduce your separate money monsters to each other, define for each other the individual money madness each of you has been carrying all this time—right into your shared relationship.

It starts with determining your current financial intimacy level, calculating your Financial Intimacy Quotient (FIQ). You'll do it by answering a set of questions for a possible total score of 11. Try answering the questions separately at first—in separate rooms, not just across a table from one another. You'll quickly note how close or distant your perceptions of your own financial intimacy are. That alone might get a conversation going.

Your Financial Intimacy Quotient	
Question (points for yes answers)	Your Points
Have you and your spouse or partner shared with one another your separate childhood money messages, money histories, and money educations? (3)	
Do you know your combined monthly cash flow—and do you discuss it regularly with your spouse or partner? (2)	
Do you know your own and your spouse's or partner's money madness and money monster? (2)	
Do you both know and have you told one another your separate and combined current net worth—that is, assets and liabilities? (I)	
Have you and your spouse or partner ever sat down to discuss your current financial picture, your separate and joint financial goals, intentions, and priorities? (2)	

Do you regularly tell your spouse or partner about purchases, investments, charitable gifts? (1)	
Total FIQ (out of possible total of 11)	

Your total FIQ score is a reliable measure of how far you need to go to improve your financial intimacy, deepen your relationship, and enhance your sex life. Because we're all birds of a feather when it comes to financial intimacy, I've divided the descriptions of what the scores say about you as a couple into four avian types, as follows:

+ *The Ostriches.* If you scored from 0 to 3 on the financial intimacy quiz, you have your head in the sand. It's clear that you and your partner know very little about either yourselves or one another where money is concerned. The good news is that the sky is the limit for you both; you have so much to learn about and share with one another: money histories, childhood money messages, money monsters, and the resulting money madness.

It won't be easy, and it will take time. Pace yourself. Just as you wouldn't start a weight-lifting program by bench-pressing 500 pounds on day one, ease into the process of lifting your head out of the sand. Begin with what's easy, open gently to one another, and work your way step by step into the deepest secrets.

+ *The Woodpeckers.* If you scored from 4 to 6, then for all the noise, you're not communicating very well as a couple. Woodpecker couples talk a good game when it comes to openness, but it's often more rat-a-tat-tat than reality. Their money conversations tend to be superficial and brief—as if money were a matter of logistics, not something central to life. In so doing, they're cheating both their love life and their money life. Commit now to making money a part of your relationship and to raising your FIQ, and both your love and your money will grow.

- *The Meadowlarks.* An FIQ of between 7 and 9 is impressive. It shows you're a couple whose finances and love are flowing lyrically—most of the time. Something, however, is keeping you from scoring a 10 or 11. You are holding back on something—some secret you don't want your spouse or partner to know about. Maybe it was how much you spent last week, or the actual lowdown on your net worth. This is the one missing ingredient that is keeping you and your spouse or partner from being totally in tune with one another. Make it your mission to disclose the secret and close the gap in your FIQ by the end of this year. When you do, you won't believe the music you'll make together.
- *The Great Horned Owls.* If you scored 10 or 11, congratulations. You are the role model for all couples. Powerfully together, alert to one another's needs, mates for life, you are together reaping the abundance—both financial and romantic—that comes from having such a high FIQ. Enjoy!

Time for Fledglings to Take Wing

As for you ostriches, woodpeckers, and meadowlarks, you all have your work cut out for you—to one extent or another. I've organized it into an eight-step program. Take as much time as you need for each step—a week per step is probably sensible. If that sounds like a long time, it really isn't. After all, the barriers to intimacy that your money madness has built have very possibly been there for years. Every time you weren't entirely truthful about how much the sweater cost, every time you used the college fund for just one more flier on a stock tip, every time you drove to the bank in the next town to withdraw cash from your own secret personal account, every time you made a big money decision without consulting your spouse, those barriers got bigger, stronger, higher.

So it will take time to break them down, and the process, which is challenging, should be deliberate. Move from one step to the next only when you feel ready to. Take the time you need to listen to one another, and watch your relationship flourish.

I can promise you two things, however, about the time you do spend on this program:

First, it will be some of the best time you and your spouse or partner have ever spent. You'll get to know one another in whole new ways, you'll rediscover what you love in one another and fall in love all over again, you'll free yourself from your secrets and provide your relationship with a booster shot of passion.

Second, you'll find that money can actually be something of an aphrodisiac. You've got a lifetime to peel away the layers of money madness from each of your lives. As you do, you'll discover all sorts of new, interesting, wonderful things about each other. You'll hear yourself talking easily about anxieties, disappointments, desires you have never expressed before—maybe even to yourself. You'll open parts of yourself through revelation and surrender that you might never even have known were there. It's what I promised you at the start of this chapter: money talk as the new foreplay.

Step I
Share Your Money Histories

Set aside 30 minutes a day for at least the next week to learn about one another's money histories. Block out the time on both your calendars now. These are important meetings—as important as a summons by the boss, for example, or a commitment to your oldest friend—and you'll want to approach them with the same seriousness, respect, and eagerness you would reserve for such meetings.

And while it's certainly okay to have the conversation in the comfort of your home, many couples find it more exciting—even romantic—to seek out the neutral turf of a restaurant or quiet park bench. I know couples who have swapped houses for the evening so each couple can share their money histories in a fresh environment.

The conversation you have during these 30 minutes a day will consist of much the same kind of exploration you—and maybe both of you—did separately back in Chapter 3: a way to evoke the memories of what it was like to grow up in your household as far as money was concerned.

A good starting point for the conversation is this: "The first time I remember money being an issue or a factor in my life is . . ." Whether the memory that surfaces is a specific event or a gradual realization or a financial transaction, make sure that it gives rise to a real conversation—a two-way talk between two equal partners—and make sure that the talk stays in the realm of feeling, not value judgments or explanations.

To ensure this, it may be helpful to structure the 30 minutes, and here's a suggestion for how to do that:

1. Spouse/Partner 1 relates his or her money story: 10 minutes.
2. Spouse/Partner 2 responds with feedback: 5 minutes.
3. Spouse/Partner 2 relates his or her money story: 10 minutes.
4. Spouse/Partner 1 responds with feedback: 5 minutes.

A Feedback Primer

It's a good idea always to begin the feedback part of the conversation with a restatement of what was heard. For one thing, that forces both of you to listen. In addition, however, hearing your own memories played back to you by someone else provides that all-important distance from the emotional charge of the memory, and that's the first step to eventual healing. When your spouse or partner says to you, "I hear in what you say that your parents always wanted to have more money," that can go a long way toward explaining why you yourself feel your self-worth is bound up with your financial worth—and why childhood emotions are governing your adult money behavior.

But the feedback needs to go a step beyond recitation of the other's money memory. The spouse or partner providing the feedback should also relate his or her emotional reaction to the other's story. Here's how to do that; just fill in the blanks of this sentence: "When you said _____, I felt _____." For example, "When you said your parents always wanted to have more money, I felt anger toward them."

Again, it's important to provide this feedback in terms of the feeling, not the content. After all, it's *feelings* that are at the heart of our money madness. That is the perspective that should prevail in this conversation, not a judgment on or analysis of the event. The tack to take is "When you said your father withheld your allowance when you were eight, I felt sadness," not "Your father was dead wrong to withhold your allowance from you." Hearing somebody else acknowledge the feeling gives you permission to do the same; you open the door to the feeling, and you let the money monster in. And as we know, once you've invited him in, he no longer rules you.

Step 2
Crunch the Numbers

What's your money situation? Do you know?

As an investor, you wouldn't take seriously a company that couldn't produce an accurate report on how much it spends each month, not to mention a statement of the corporation's net worth. Yet it never fails to amaze me that households, which are mini-companies that operate in much the same way as corporations, rarely have this kind of information—whether the household is headed by a couple or an individual. Producing such a report, as you'll do in this next step, can lead to insights about your values, preferences, and aspirations that will be downright eye-opening and potentially life-changing to both you and your partner.

Start by filling out the cash flow and household net worth templates—together. What you're trying to do is just estimate the numbers and come to some sort of agreement. Have fun. This is not a statistical exercise; the aim is to see the big picture together.

The first template is a portrait of your family's monthly cash flow—expenses, net take-home pay, and the difference between the two. We look at net pay because that's the real income, the cash that's available for spending—not your pretax salary, a hefty portion of which goes to the government in taxes. It's something people tend to disregard when they think about their money, but in fact, there can be a big difference between a yearly salary figure and the amount of money you actually have on hand. For example, if you think of an annual salary of $90,000 as translating into a monthly cash supply of

$7,500—that is, $90,000 divided by 12 months—you'll be sorely mistaken, and chances are good you'll overspend as a result. So in figuring monthly cash, it's essential to think take-home pay, not pretax salary or wages.

The second template asks you for a standard statement of net worth of the corporation that is your family household. As with any corporation, that means tracking all your assets and liabilities and subtracting the latter from the former. If you can, fill out your net worth for the last three years, ending this past December 31, for reasons that will become clear in a moment.

In the meantime, you'll probably learn through filling out these templates together that you and your partner or spouse have very different perceptions about how much money comes into your household and where it comes from, as well as about how much money leaves your household, where it goes, and how much remains—if any—out of the money that comes in. I've seen husbands go speechless when they see what it costs to clothe their children. I've seen wives correct their husbands—gently or not so gently—about what the husbands consider their "minimal" expenditures on gear for golf, hunting, fishing, racquetball, and so on. I've seen couples catch their breath when they realize what their dining-out bill comes to on a monthly basis or what the gardening and maintenance actually cost.

You may also find that the exercise throws some light on the balance or imbalance of power—financial power—in your relationship. Maybe only one of you knows where to locate the various documents that show you the value of your household assets and liabilities. Maybe the other has a far better handle on what day-to-day commodities cost in this current economy. Most couples learn that each partner brings a particular money expertise to the table, and that can be a spur to equalizing the money power in the relationship. You might also find that your money behaviors actually complement one another: A saver falls for a spender, or a hoarder and a giver end up as a couple.

The end result can only be greater sharing and deeper trust between you—a big step on the road to financial intimacy.

Your Household's Monthly Cash Flow

FIXED SPENDING	MONTHLY VALUE
Housing	
Mortgage/rent	
Property taxes and homeowner's/renter's insurance	
Savings for long-term repairs/improvements	
Maintenance and cleaning	
Utilities	
Other	
Housing total	
Household	
Savings for goals	
Groceries	
Medical/dental	
Education	
Credit card/other loan payments	
Attorney, CPA, and other professional fees	
Household necessities (pet care, toiletries, dry cleaning, personal care, and so on)	
Computer/cell phone	
Health, life, disability, and long-term care insurance	
Other	
Household total	

FIXED SPENDING	MONTHLY VALUE
Transportation	
Car payment	
Car insurance	
Gas	
Parking	
Maintenance, repairs	
Public transportation	
Other	
Transportation total	
Total fixed expenses	
FLEXIBLE SPENDING	
Clothing	
Home furnishings	
Entertainment/vacations	
Charity	
Gifts	
Fitness	
Personal growth	
Other	
Total flexible expenses	
TOTAL EXPENSES (total fixed expenses + total flexible expenses)	
TOTAL INCOME (net take-home pay + investment income)	
NET CASH FLOW (total income — total expenses)	

Your Household Net Worth

Assets	December 31		
	3 Years Ago	2 Years Ago	Last Year
Liquid assets			
Bank accounts			
CDs			
Money markets			
Total liquid assets			
Investment assets			
Brokerage accounts			
Mutual funds			
Business assets			
Total investment assets			
Retirement assets			
IRAs			
Employer-sponsored retirement plan			
Total retirement assets			
Real estate assets			
Primary residence			
Second or vacation home			
Rental properties			
Total real estate assets			
Total assets			

	December 31		
Liabilities	**3 Years Ago**	**2 Years Ago**	**Last Year**
Personal loans			
Credit cards			
Mortgage(s)/home equity loans			
Business loans			
Student loans			
Other			
Total liabilities			
TOTAL NET WORTH (total assets—total liabilities)			

With your cash flow statement staring you in the face, you now know where your money goes. With your net worth statement down on paper, you now know all the things of value you own, all the debts you owe, and the difference between the two—and whether and by how much your net worth is either positive or negative.

What's more, if you've been able to put down your net worth for the three-year period ending last or this December 31, you'll get an accurate picture of what's really happening over time. For example, you may have assumed from your brokerage statements that your net worth was going up, but when you see that your debt has also been rising, that changes the picture considerably.

Look at these two templates together. These numbers don't lie, and the chances are they show you a truth that is different from what you thought, or assumed, or expected. They tell you what *is*—where you are in your family's money life. Now it's time to look at where you want to be.

Step 3
Co-Design Your Joint Money Life

Is the picture painted by your cash flow and net worth statements the picture you want to see? Is the money life you live the one you want to live—one in tune with your values and convictions and preferences?

The numbers in your monthly cash flow statement might show, for example, that you value your house much more than you value dining out, entertainment, or going on vacation. It's right there in black and white: Of the money available each month, lots of it is spent on the house, very little on vacations. That's the truth of how you spend. Is it the truth of how you *want* to spend? Is it an accurate representation of what you value as a couple—your spending intentions? That's what you need to determine in Step 3. It's your chance to co-design the money life you want to have together.

My suggestion is to use a colored pen to highlight what you want to change. Start by flagging the numbers that look "wrong"—out of sync with your values or predilections. Then consider together what you want the numbers to be—*your spending intentions*—and set this down as a range between the least amount you think is desirable and the most you want to spend in each category. Keep in mind, of course, that outgo must not exceed inflow.

In doing Step 3, you will find you are taking back control of your spending from your money monsters. You are making yourselves the co-CEOs of the corporation that is your household, creating cash flow and net worth templates that represent the kind of household you'd like to have and the kind of family you want to be.

This Can Be Painful, But It Pays Off in Intimacy

My financial clients and my workshop participants agree unanimously that this process of facing your financial situation together is the most powerful change agent they've ever undertaken in both their money life and their relationship with their partner. (It's also the exercise that they invariably resist the most.) It is likely to show you how little you both know about your actual money situation. By requiring you to come together to discuss the situation, the process prompts you to analyze your spending, your possessions, and your debts and thus to look closely at one another's values. And by designing your money life together, you automatically share your values, yield to one another, compromise on the issue of control, and shed any kind of victimhood. The process itself is an amazing catalyst for intimacy.

But candor compels me to warn you that it can also be a painful process. Discrepancies between your separate perceptions can stir stressful feelings. Instead of arguing over these feelings or over-analyzing them or criticizing them—which we've all done, to no purpose—the idea is to make one another aware of the feelings. That is what the process is all about—airing these feelings so you can resolve the separate perceptions, and in so doing resolve the numbers.

But do it compassionately. If you hear your spouse assert that his monthly discretionary spending is $25, and you know there is a closet in the basement that looks like the inside of a sporting goods or hardware store—with a price tag you can only guess at—remember that his spending is a kind of money madness that results from his childhood money history. It's not about you; it's his money madness at work.

Be gentle as you help him resolve the discrepancy and arrive at the truth. Start by acknowledging that both of you are ruled in your money behavior by a madness deriving from your money past. Express with compassion your understanding of his money past. Offer up a weakness of your own—the pashmina scarf you couldn't resist. Express your confusion. Only then do you mention that you know about the brand-new bicycle gear and the fly-fishing rod with tackle in the basement—and do so in the context of a suggestion that you work together, through your separate money madnesses, to get control of your household money situation. Instead of accusing, therefore, you're showing a commitment to the two of you dealing with your finances.

"We both have money madness," you might begin, "and I know our money madness comes from our childhood money histories. I understand, Tom, that you were always told that you don't have to worry about money, and it's led to a carefree attitude that's often wonderful. I love the generous side of you, but I sometimes struggle with the overspending part of it. I know that I overspend too; that scarf I bought the other day was way out of line.

"I do feel sad that few boundaries on spending were set for you when you were a kid. But I'm also confused when you say you spend $25 a month for discretionary spending when I've seen the outdoor gear in the basement closet. Given that we're both committed to financial success, let's talk about it."

Be aware again that you are only aiming for a rough approximation of the numbers, not for an accounting that is exact down to the penny. Again, the goal of this exercise is to increase your awareness of your true financial situation, to shed light on a part of your relationship that has been in the dark, and in that way to reduce stress over the long term.

It may be a shock for both of you to see how much money you are actually spending—and/or to see what you are spending it *on*. You may be stunned when you see the truth about the value of your assets vis-à-vis your liabilities. But it is precisely these eye-openers that are the essential starting points for undoing your separate money madnesses and rethinking and redesigning your joint money life—an intimacy-building exercise if ever there was one.

Now Share Your Values

You need to talk.

Yes, I know you've started to. You've been sharing your money histories and your perceptions of your household spending and your net worth. And certainly, as every couple does, you talk about money all the time, as in: "Don't forget to stop at the ATM on your way home" or "The kids need money for this or that school event" or "I can't believe you swiped the quarters I've been collecting for the car wash!" But now it's time to talk about your money values.

No doubt you've shared your values about work, spiritual matters, politics, sex, and the best movies you've ever seen. You've discussed what matters to each of you. You've talked about the convictions that guide your behavior in all life's key areas. But I'll bet you've never had one of those deep across-the-table or across-the-pillow conversations about the nitty-gritty of your money values.

This is another not-so-easy process, so I've structured a discussion agenda for the month. As you did in Step 1 when you shared your money history, set aside time for these discussions. You'll want at least half an hour for each discussion—probably more—so a good idea is to schedule these talks for evening, when the day's routine is over. Think about going out to dinner for the discussion. That will give you the time and space you need, and the agenda will provide the focus.

Step 4
Talk About the Role of Money

"What role should money play in our lives?" may not be the most felicitous opening line to a discussion, but however you begin, this is a conversation that needs to take place. After all, what is this thing that generates so much fear and longing—and that the two of you aren't talking about in your relationship? What role do the two of you want money to play in the life you share? Only in talking it through will you be able to come to some shared acknowledgment of the role each of you sees money playing in your shared life. From such a starting point, a shared acceptance of the role it should play may emerge.

First of all, how does each of you see money? Is it a medium of exchange? Measure of success? Commodity? All of the above? Is money a virtue? A vice? Neutral? You've already talked to one another about your money histories, childhood money messages, and individual money madnesses. What have you learned from those discussions that can help you plot a joint definition of money—a shared vision of its role in your lives?

Second, what should money mean for you as a couple? Is it freedom? Security? Self-worth? Adventure? A responsibility you'd just as soon shirk? Protection?

In other words, what kinds of problems should money solve—and what kinds of problems should it not solve? What kind of a tool is it?

Ask yourselves and one another if money is there for keeping you afloat or for funding an attempt to make millions.

Ask yourselves whether you are willing to sacrifice time for money and today's gratification for tomorrow's. How willing?

Should money be used to help relatives or friends in need? What about relatives or friends not in need? Should you use it to subsidize others—for example, to take friends on a vacation they could not afford on their own because you value their company?

By the same token, should we accept financial help if we need it? And, therefore, should we be willing to discuss our financial successes and failures openly with others?

Finally, articulate how you will stay in love regardless of the vagaries of your financial situation and the world's economy.

Surely two people who love one another and are making a life together should take time to explore together how they feel about money and what role they want it to play in their lives.

Step 5
Discuss Core Money Transactions

Within that context, begin by talking to one another about your values vis-à-vis saving, investing, giving to charity, being taxed, even paying for your home—the core ways money flows through your lives.

For example, how much, if any, should you be saving—and to what purpose? Do you need to put money aside as a reserve for possible emergencies? Or do you want to build up savings for your dream home, for the kids' college education, for retirement?

What about investing? Are you comfortable with the amount you're investing? What do you hope to gain from your investments— a knockout punch or steady growth? How does each of you react to both bull and bear markets?

What are your family's values when it comes to charitable giving? Do you want to give to whoever gets to you first; to the needy causes and people who approach you on the street; or through a planned, proactive, businesslike strategy of philanthropy?

How about taxes? Just about everyone seeks every advantage she can get in preparing her tax return. How aggressively will you seek that advantage? Is it worth hiring an expert to find every possible loophole?

Whether you buy or rent your home (more on this in Chapter 8), it is probably the biggest-ticket expense you have. How does each of you regard your home—as a retirement plan, a statement about your lifestyle, a shelter? Are you both comfortable in your home or do you want it to be something else?

These are key issues in the life of a family, a household, a relationship. Your intimacy as a couple grows stronger and deeper as you thrash out your feelings and thoughts on these issues and come to a place either of shared values or of acknowledgment of your different values. Such an acknowledgment is the first step toward becoming a cheerleader of your partner's distinct values.

Step 6
Set a Money Example for Your Children

Remember how you received your childhood money message? It's no different for *your* kids. Where money is concerned, kids learn from how you behave with money more than what you say about it. When I noticed that my son's allowance shoe box wasn't in its usual place, and I heard myself questioning him about it with some tension in my voice, his puzzled look and casual suggestion that "we'll find it tomorrow" stunned me. I quickly realized I was transmitting the same message of desperation about money I had received at his age—and I quickly clammed up. So it's important to talk about the values you want your children to have in regard to money—the childhood money messages you want to transmit to them.

Of course, whatever the values you want to impart, you'll need to mirror them yourself. You can't just provide a lecture along with the monthly allowance; it's the things you do that really teach kids—how you spend, how you give, what you say and don't say about the neighbors' new car or the McMansion going up across the street.

Wherever your actions lead, that's where your kids will follow. So talk now about how to make sure you live the money values you want your children to have.

Step 7
Share a Secret

For me, it's investing. Maybe it's because of my background. Maybe I just love the process. Maybe it's my nature. I don't know. But I finally figured out that it's important to me to have the freedom to make some investments on my own, without checking in with my wife.

So we talked about it, and Janine said that was fine, then asked me to let her know the status of the investments once a quarter. "And in return," she added, "I'd like to make my clothing purchases without any questions." A deal.

It was liberating to be able to share the secret that I was making these investments by myself and clandestinely—I didn't have to pretend anymore—and it deepened my sense of intimacy with Janine as well. But it wasn't enough just to share the secret; it was important to assign some accountability for it as well, so together, we came up with a dollar ceiling for these "secret" investments.

Your assignment in Step 7 is to share the secret of the separate bank account your spouse can't access or of the credit card you're keeping to yourself or of the component of your money madness you can't seem to give up but no longer want to act out behind the back of the person you live with. Make it clear as you come clean that you own this behavior and that it derives from your childhood money messages; it has nothing to do with your partner. Money madness has dictated both your subversive behavior and your inability to communicate it.

The person hearing the secret has to understand that this is the partner's money madness, not a comment on the relationship. That is, it isn't about you; it isn't about love and trust; it's about behavior deriving from money messages your partner received in childhood.

You'll find that because money secrets diminish intimacy, the disclosure alone will enhance your intimacy with your spouse or partner. But that's not all it will do. Once you've shared the secret of your behavior, the driving need to do the behavior will diminish. When I told all to Janine, it became the starting point for a conversation in which we both learned a lot about each other. I learned that she trusted me, and that trust made the secrecy as unnecessary as it was untenable.

It's like outing a covert agent; the agent's effectiveness is gone. Similarly, **the money monster operates like a covert agent. He doesn't like the light of revelation; he flourishes in darkness. Your spouse's knowledge and approval of your "secret" deny the money monster a large measure of his power.**

Step 8
Divergent Dreams? Start Resolving Them Now

Jennifer has always dreamed of living in a tropical paradise; her husband, Sam, wants to move to the middle of Manhattan.

Paul is working 24/7 so he can retire early and kick back totally; his wife, Alice, can't wait to dive back into the workforce once the kids are grown and gone.

Mike assumes that he and Maggie will just leave everything to be equally divided among their three children; Maggie thinks that inherited wealth will rob the kids of a vigor and strength that are important to their character and would rather bequeath what they have to reducing global warming.

Anne Watts and I see it in our couples workshops all the time: divergent dreams about the future. When you first meet and are in the honeymoon phase, disparate visions of where and how you'll live in 40 or 50 years seem remote, and the disparity appears unimportant. But as you grow older, as you grow in your profession or as your children focus your eyes on the future, as you perhaps begin to feel the first diminutions of energy and power that come with age, you begin to wonder what you will do about this disparity when the future arrives.

But if you put off tackling the issue, it may be way too late. Certainly, there is a tendency to wait it out, to assume that the future will take care of itself. That's fine, but what if it doesn't?

The good news is that these divergent dreams represent an opportunity to enhance intimacy. Separate, unshared, unlistened to, unaffirmed, these disparate visions become polarizing. If he gets to have his dream, I lose mine, one of you may think. If her vision of living on a tropical island prevails, my vision of living in the city is shattered forever. Each of you digs your way deeper into a rigid position. Communication dries up. Resentment takes root. The issue, now bigger and more stubborn than ever, gets shoved back in the closet.

That's why it's so important to make this issue a part of freeing yourselves from your money madness. When you do, several things happen, as Anne and I have found time and again in our workshops.

First of all, without money madness, you are able to listen in a different way. When you have sent your money monster packing, you find—perhaps as a surprise—that you are less attached to conventional thinking about where to live, when to retire, how to vacation, what constitutes financial security. Released from the standard fixations—we have to retire at 65, we must move to/away from the city, we need a million dollars to do it—a real conversation becomes possible.

Listening without preconceived notions enables understanding and acceptance of the other's dream. You begin to get it, to understand why the tropical island seems so important or desirable. You might come to see the origin of the dream and feel a new understanding of your partner. Now you can affirm that you get it, and in doing so, you validate your partner's dream.

And then a funny thing begins to happen. Once you've accepted and affirmed your partner's dream, your partner has space to affirm your dream. Resentment fades, replaced by trust. And both of you find that maybe your tightly held dreams are not so rigid after all; maybe there's a middle ground, or a way to blend the two, or something else altogether you both could devise.

For example, maybe Jennifer and Sam can work out a plan whereby they live in New York for a year and on the Gulf Coast for a year. Then they could together devise a future they could both enjoy.

So take this issue up now, let the tensions surface, and start to resolve them.

How? Simple. Look at yourselves from the outside. Give yourselves other names—say, Adam and Eve. And give Adam and Eve your divergent dreams. Now ask yourselves how you can help both Adam and Eve achieve their dreams.

Be creative. I had a client couple—Ben and Barbara—who had wildly divergent goals for their investments. Barbara wanted to save money for their children's college education. Ben thought the kids should work and borrow their way through college as he had done; he wanted to invest in real estate instead. Their solution? They bought a beach house and agreed they would sell it when the time came to pay for the kids' education.

It worked. Financially, the proceeds from the house provided the bulk of tuition and costs for their three children, although the kids did have to borrow a bit to make up the difference. As far as Ben and Barbara's relationship was concerned, the win was even more substantive. Each found that by rooting for one another's goals, they freed each other to see other possibilities. And by affirming one another's dreams, they created a kind of intimacy they had not known before.

So how would I rate Ben and Barbara's FIQ? A perfect 11.

Life Among the Great Horned Owls

"Every time I made an investment and didn't tell Janine about it felt like a weight on my shoulders." That's what I wrote a few pages back when I was describing my own FIQ, which at the time was probably somewhere around sub-ostrich. The weight contained several pounds of loneliness (I was doing this investing all by myself), several pounds of fear (all the responsibility was on me and what if it didn't pan out?), and several pounds of outright shame (I felt dishonest doing this behind my wife's back). Yes, I controlled the money in the relationship, but all that produced was a feeling of betrayal and separation—not what you want in a relationship.

Today, all that has changed. And money was the transforming mechanism.

Divergent dreams about a vacation proved to be the catalyst. Janine wanted us all to go to London. It's the city of her dreams, a destination of sheer magic for her, and she wanted us all to share her love of the place.

That's when my old money monster, never far under the surface, raised his ugly head. My argument to Janine was that because we both felt it was important for the kids to learn Spanish, we ought to begin the instruction by taking them, young as they are, to Mexico. In this way, we would open their minds and ears to a new culture that expresses itself in an entirely different language, so that by the time they were ready to begin serious language study, they would have a sense of Spanish.

That's what I said anyway, when Janine and I talked—with increasing irritation with one another—about our separate ideas for the vacation. The truth of course was that I was right back in my old money madness. I simply couldn't stomach the idea of spending money "unproductively," as I saw it, on a frivolous trip to London when there was a perfectly good utilitarian purpose closer to hand—a shorter trip to nearby Mexico, where the kids could start getting Spanish into their ears so they could grow up to have more career options. That was the crass, unvarnished bottom line.

We argued. Some couples don't argue at all about money; some argue quite fiercely; Janine and I usually argue by becoming distant from one another. Caught once again in the grip of my money monster, I couldn't even hear her vision about London, much less affirm it; all I heard was that threatening reality that money would be spent to achieve the vision. The more I couldn't hear her, of course, the more she stuck to her guns. It went on for two years.

That seemed a long time, so one day I decided to do something about it. I set out to break the pattern by assuming the opposite role, turning myself into a person who loved London as much as Janine does. I remembered what I cherished about the city, and as I did so, awareness began to kick in. Oh, I said to myself, this is my old friend the money monster knocking at the door, telling me to be afraid that money will flow away from me and that my security and survival are threatened. I opened it and invited him in—and as always happens, once I decided to stop wrestling with him, he lost his power and faded from view. Even as I write this, I can feel the tension the monster caused in me in this stand-off with my wife, and I can again experience the release of that tension—the lightness and space—when the deflated, emasculated money monster simply dissolved away.

I could now see the wisdom in Janine's dream for this vacation. Seeing the wisdom, it was easy to affirm her vision and validate her dream, different though it was from mine.

"I want to talk about London," I said one day. "I want to be more open to your idea."

That's when she startled me by replying: "And I'm becoming more interested in teaching the kids Spanish."

Affirming each other's visions, we were both able to shift off our rigid, polarizing positions. It opened up a whole bunch of conversations.

Another change took place after I confessed to her that I wanted to continue making secret, slightly risky investments on my own. As she asked, I began to talk to Janine about them every quarter. I came to value the wisdom and objectivity she brought to the conversation. I found that I was making fewer risky investments, that I felt less of a thrill in doing so, as if my money monster were finally tiring of setting me up for that elusive grand slam in the market. As a result, I became much calmer.

Janine and I also talk a lot about philanthropy these days. We have determined that we will do half of our giving jointly and that each of us will do 25 percent on our own. That half prompts a lot of discussion, a lot of sharing of values, a lot of intimacy.

The last change I've seen since we've been working on our FIQ is in spending. Now that we make our purchases together, I'm buying more wisely.

In all these areas—investing, giving, spending—I used to be in sole control. And I was always worried—worried about how much Janine was giving to such-and-such charity, or about keeping from her the details of my latest real estate investment, or about how to explain our tax situation.

We are co-CEOs now, and the household we manage runs much better. We are co-reviewers of our income, assets, liabilities, taxes. Co-decision makers. It means there is trust between us; there has to be trust, and there is. And that makes everything better—our love life, our friendship with each other, our parenting.

We just simply know one another better. We've gone well past the normal logistical conversations spouses invariably must have: "How was your day?" "Did you remember to pick up the cleaning?" "Jeremy has a doctor's appointment tomorrow." We've shared our money histories, looked hard at the real numbers of our money life, sifted our separate and joint values, divulged secrets, affirmed one another's dreams even if they clashed with our own. We have learned a lot about each other, and money was the teacher.

And as for the passion in our marriage, I will tell you this: It is much more fun to be a great horned owl than an ostrich.

CHAPTER 6

The Rainbow Portfolio™

Madness-Free Investing—The Boring Way to Make *More* Money

Every winter here in northern California, my neighbors and I begin to look forward to our great annual pastime—planting tomatoes in the spring. As we know, and as agricultural experts and local farmers confirm, the time to do so is in May, when the threat of a late, tomato-killing frost is long past.

Yet every March, when the temperature first creeps again into the 70s and all of a sudden it feels almost like summer, there are always a few people who decide to plant their tomatoes *now*.

I've been one of those people, and I know what it feels like. After months of surprisingly chilly temperatures, the sudden warmth suffuses one's bones. The sun is boldly bright. It becomes absolutely clear in our minds that this year, the timing of the seasons really is different, and that summer has arrived to stay.

The promise is delicious—and virtually irresistible: Plant now and steal a march on everybody else, seize the advantage, stand out with tomatoes that bloom first, showcasing your garden ahead of all the other gardens in the neighborhood—and getting to eat tomatoes sooner than everybody else. Why wait till May, with its boring predictability of a good, solid harvest, when you can take a chance on winning the glory of early and conspicuous gain?

So despite the fact that we know better, we are beguiled into the conviction that the seeds we plant now will bloom brilliantly into lavishly red, luscious tomatoes we can point to with pride and eat with gusto.

No one I know can remember the last time early planted tomatoes survived. Old-timers say it has happened, but not in recent memory. On the contrary: There is invariably a frost sometime between the seduction of March and the reality of May, and the tomatoes fail.

If only we tomato growers could learn simply to witness the enticements of sun and warmth passively—and not yield to them—we would wait till May before planting, and we would thus ensure ourselves a nice, juicy crop summer after summer after summer, year in, year out.

If only investors could do the same—witness the temptation of a "system" that can beat the odds, of a tip that promises to make a killing, of their own desire to outsmart the market, without actually yielding to that temptation—they too could enjoy a nice, steady gain in earnings decade after decade. And if they did that, then they would accumulate more money than even their fantasies could have imagined.

The Rainbow Portfolio

The Rainbow Portfolio is a structured methodology for doing that very thing—making more money from investing than you ever thought possible, simply by doing the opposite of what your money monster typically wants you to do. Actually, with the Rainbow Portfolio, you do just about nothing. And because it's hard to get stressed over nothing, the Rainbow Portfolio also rids your life of a lot of the anxiety people tend to attach to their investing, thus increasing your time for other pursuits. (That's why I actually think that "boring" is sexy.)

If this book were about physical fitness, the Rainbow Portfolio would represent the "maintenance phase." Having labored hard to *get* into shape through the difficult work of the awareness cure, this is the part of the program you follow pretty much by rote to *stay* in shape. It's a ready-made, almost automatic structure in which the dots are already well connected to keep your money monster at bay.

In this chapter, I tell you what the Rainbow Portfolio is, how it evolved out of my own pain and failure, and the three simple principles that make it work: diversification—including an emphasis on what I call small-and-boring or the small-value asset class—witness discipline, and rebalancing.

I'll also show you how to create your own personal Rainbow Portfolio, a structure you can build, in concert with your broker or advisor if you like, to make more money than you can now imagine out of your investments in a madness-free way—even if it's no fun talking about those investments at dinner parties.

As someone who has been around the block a few times where money is concerned, I know that there are few guarantees in life, but I'm confident in guaranteeing you this: Follow the Rainbow Portfolio, and you will succeed as an investor in a whole new way, and you will make room in your life to pursue myriad new paths to happiness and fulfillment.

Let's begin by taking a look at the close relationship between investing and money madness.

Investing Is Thrilling—But Noisy

What is it about investing that sends so many people—many of them perfectly rational, sober, even stolid in their attitudes—into a frenzy of excitement that can sometimes approach hysteria? We know the answer, of course. It's money madness. It's emotion—the equivalent of the tomato grower's yearning for summer—not the facts of market history and money behavior. For those facts are clear—and they have been clear for generations.

Indeed, it's over generations that the story of investing must be told, for investing is, virtually by definition, a long-term proposition. But, of course, if the pontificating pundits and analysts and financial experts ever covered the real story of investing, it would be so boring nobody would pay any attention:

January 1, 2009. The six o'clock news: "We turn now to the monotonous and predictably dull latest results from Wall Street for the S&P 500 index, the world-renowned statistical composite for tracking change in the U.S. stock market. Over the last 10 years—from December 31, 1998, to December 31, 2008—the S&P 500 index rose. Again. Just as it did for the previous 10 years, and for the 10 years before that, and for the 10 years before that. Remember to tune in for our next stock market report on January 1, 2010."

Had there been a report every New Year's Day on how the S&P

500 did in the previous decade, then every decade since 1926—with two exceptions—that report would have been positive. The exceptions? The 10-year period from 1929 to 1938 saw a total market decline of 8.6 percent, and the 10 years from 1930 to 1939 saw the market basically flat—actually, down by 1 percent. I would remind readers that those decades included perhaps the most brutal years of the global Great Depression, when the world's economy sank to its lowest point in recorded history. The heavy losses associated with the stock market crash of 1929, giving birth to the legendary image of investors jumping out of windows high above Wall Street, were indeed intense. But the losses were also limited in duration—thus confirming the truth that investing needs to be a long-term proposition, measured in decades rather than a year at a time.

Still, what these figures tell us is that 97.3 percent of the time, the New Year's Day headline from the stock market says exactly the same thing: For the recent decade, stocks were up. (It's mid-2008 as I write this, so anything might still happen in the last months of the decade ending December 31, 2008. But the fact is that even if the current financial crisis causes a stock market crash worse than 1929, that percentage would drop only from 97.3 percent of the time to 96 percent.) World War II, revolution in China, the Korean and Vietnam wars, the oil embargo, the AIDS pandemic, turmoil in the Middle East, upheaval in Africa, avian flu, two Iraq wars, the attacks of September 11, 2001, the ups and downs of your own life: Through it all, the S&P 500 has remained undeterred—and on a positive upward track.

If the financial news networks were issuing these New Year's Day decade reports every year, we would have heard 74 of them as this book goes to press. This would also mean that 89 percent of the time since 1935, stock market investing realized a higher return than did investing in one-month Treasury bills, which people often choose as a safe haven for their money. And it would mean that 91 percent of the time since 1935, stocks beat inflation, meaning that yields from stock investments held their purchasing power despite rising prices. Treasury bills did so only 64 percent of the time.

Is there another area of life with a record of such consistency? Is there anything in *your* life that has continued to increase in value decade after decade the way the stock market has? Your job, your car, your health, your favorite restaurant, your marriage, your golf game, your libido: As barometers go, is any one of them as *reliably* positive and upward-tending in value? No way. (Sure, if you looked at five-year periods instead of decades, there would be a few more downturns; but if you looked at 15-year periods, there would be none.)

What these rock-bottom facts about the consistency and reliability of the stock market tell us is a success story. Yet that success story is one of the dirty little secrets of investing. Drowning it out is an incredible amount of noise, the decibel level of which has been rising steadily over the years.

What do I mean by *noise*? I'm talking about all the articles in financial magazines with titles like "Five Mutual Funds You Must Buy *Now*."

I'm talking about all those compelling ads in print and on TV—that perfectly groomed couple in their very fit-looking late 50s rafting the rapids with their grandchildren, to whom they are no doubt imparting the valuable lesson of investing in the retirement fund so cleverly being hawked—its past performance being only selectively revealed, if at all.

I'm talking about all the cable television "financial" shows, which have turned short-term market volatility into a form of entertainment. With the ticker tape crawling along the bottom of the screen and constantly moving charts and graphs in the upper corners of the screen, we're treated to a succession of talking heads in the middle of the screen bloviating about which stocks to buy and why the market is about to tumble—all aimed at pumping up the audience and feeding them the idea that it's possible to get an edge on others with this or that stock pick.

The noise is contagious. In addition to all the static on the airwaves and in print, some investing messages come as part of your family legacy—a parent urging you to invest only in utility stocks, or to stay away from mutual funds, or to keep it simple and avoid the stock market altogether. Or maybe your friends keep begging you to buy into their start-up company, or your brother-in-law assures you that technology stocks are the path to easy money, or your spouse is positive that solar energy is the place to be. And, of course, there is always somebody at the latest dinner party warning in an authoritative-sounding voice that recession is near and the stock market is on the verge of collapse.

The noise is constant; it's 24/7. You can't go to a ball game these days without seeing the market ticker tape on the scoreboard. The latest on the Dow? That's nothing. Today, you can have reports on the FTSE, the Dax, and the Hang Seng streamed to your cell phone or BlackBerry, along with up-to-the-instant reports on a government that just fell in Asia or an oil field on fire in the Middle East.

Expert Help Is No Help at All

The reports look serious. The data sound rational, precise, scientific. But in fact, it's all geared to the emotions. It's aimed at persuading you that the market is dangerous, tricky, sneaky, wild, and unpredictable, and that you're going to need expert help if you're to make money in the market at all.

But, of course, as we've seen—as the facts make abundantly clear—the market is anything but dangerous, tricky, sneaky, wild, and unpredictable. Over the long term, it is, instead, as predictable as a sunrise, as straightforward as a Swiss train timetable. And as we will also see, it simply isn't true that you need expert help to make money in the market.

That, in fact, is the other dirty little secret of investing. Pundits like the Jim Cramers of this world, investment advisors like me, brokers, and others involved in the financial markets would like the public to believe that making money in the market takes a lot of hard work, and that we alone—thanks to our education, training, native intelligence, and intuition—have a patent on what it takes. But it just isn't so.

It has been shown conclusively[1] that, as far as the last 50 years of stock market investing is concerned, someone with two hours of training who invested in the S&P 500 index—and took no further action on the portfolio—would have performed better than the average professional investor with a Ph.D. in economics or an MBA in finance. You would not want someone with two hours of medical training to perform open-heart surgery on you, but you would honestly do as well as a professional in the stock market, if not better, if you eschewed the so-called hard work of investment management.

But the noise keeps insisting that the market is scary and slippery, and that it takes trained experts to succeed in it, and it does so by the simple expedient of targeting your emotions, activating your money madness, and stirring your money monster to action. "Quick!" the noise is telling you: "React!"—to the merger or the election results or the subprime credit crisis or whatever bit of news is streaming into your iPhone now. "Call your broker!" says your money monster. "Check in with your investment advisor!"—who just happens to have an exclusive stratagem for sneaking you past the crowds of losers to the front of the line.

The money monster delights in watching our high-priced investment advisors shift money from one asset class to another in response to a war being declared somewhere or when corporation A merges with corporation B or in the face of a catastrophic event like 9/11 or Hurricane Katrina. He thrives on our gullibility when the advisor promises that if the market is about to go down, she'll protect us by getting out in time. But all these instant responses tend to erode your investments rather than protect them. Most often, you sell to protect yourself, then re-enter the market later at a higher level—but having missed out on the gains that followed the loss you saved yourself from. You sell when the Dow is at 10,000, thus protecting yourself from its low of 8,500, but it isn't till it's at 11,000 that you get back in—thereby costing yourself 10 percent.

Bottom line? So many of these "protective" gyrations are really just so much sound and fury, and they signify little against the facts of the market's reliability and the superfluity of expertise. Even if the advisor gets it right nearly every time, the advantage can be measured in pennies at best. The gyrations churn up your emotions and send your money monster into high gear, but they don't help you make money on your investments.

There Is No Guarantee of Future Performance

I know this because I fell for it, just as I once fell for the seductions of sun and warmth in March, just as most investors still fall for the idea that you really can stand out from the crowd and beat the market.

I was a highly trained, highly credentialed investment advisor, and like the vast majority of my fellow investment advisors, I was paying big bucks for quarterly newsletters from stock-picking experts, was reading all the ratings, and kept shifting money from one fund to another in search of that edge that would put me—and my clients' portfolios—a step ahead of the market and a dollar ahead of the pack of other investors.

There was a fundamental fallacy inherent in this "research," although it eluded me at the time. The stock-picking newsletters are all about what has happened in the past—how such and such a stock fund performed last year, or over the last five years. Yet the truth is that in investing, there is no actual correlation between past record and future performance. It's not like buying a television or a car, commodities whose essential features you can measure. Knowing statistics such as how many times the TV under consideration has needed repair over the last five years, or the average yearly cost of maintenance for a particular car, or what past owners have said about the item's reliability can be an illuminating guide to future performance.

Not so with stocks. Studies show there is no predictive value in a stock's performance over the course of a year or a decade. The reason? A stock that performs well is bid up in price to the point at which the future return is diminished, and the stock reverts to the mean. Think of eBay: Its stock was bid up so high that it reached a point of untenable expectations, and the performance flatlined.

And in the case of active mutual funds—funds whose manager selects the stocks to be bought and sold on a daily basis—you are in effect "buying" the person managing the fund. That means you are buying not just that individual's intelligence and experience but also her personal money madness. And unless you know the person intimately, know her childhood money messages, understand the power of her money monster, and know which emotions sway the person to which behaviors, you're buying a pig in a poke when you invest in that fund.

If I was only dimly aware of this inherent fallacy, I was nevertheless becoming acutely aware of how costly it was to invest in these active funds. By contrast, with passive investing, the fund manager is typically trying to do one of two things. He may be trying to mimic a particular market and replicate its performance by owning a representative sample of the stocks in that market—the S&P 500 index, which means mimicking the performance of the stocks of 500 well-known large-cap U.S. companies, or the Russell 2000 index, which means mimicking the performance of 2,000 small-cap companies, to take just two common examples. These are called index funds.

Or the fund manager may be using financial ratios to slice up the market in a particular way—maybe into stocks with the lowest price-to-earnings ratio, or the smallest companies in Europe, or some such. If she's slicing, she isn't trying to replicate an index but rather to achieve high returns with a segment of the market that has a favorable track record. These are called passive funds.

Either way, in passive investing, the fund manager buys a group of stocks and holds them. An index fund manager will delete a stock from the portfolio only if and when the S&P or the Russell deletes it; a slicing fund manager drops a stock when it no longer fits the profile of the slice she has cut out of the market. Of course, expenses are incurred to buy the stocks and set up the fund, but that's about it.

In the kind of active investing I was involved in, however, fund managers constantly monitor the market, world events, and the performance of the companies represented by the stocks in their portfolios. And as they monitor, they react—to the latest hiccup in the market in Kuala Lumpur, to a change of government in Croatia, to a change of management in a company whose stock they bought a month ago. Intelligence gathering and analysis of gathered intelligence must therefore be ongoing, and that costs money; educated, trained, savvy researchers don't come cheap, and some of these fund managers employ large teams of such researchers. Most of the researchers are plugged into the world via the very latest communications technology, also not a cheap proposition; and of course, there are fees for executing the buy and sell decisions the fund managers make based on all that research. It adds up.

In time, I began to realize that if I couldn't predict how a fund manager would do in the future based on what he had done in the past, I could nevertheless be certain that the expenses the fund manager charged were eating into whatever booty his actions were realizing—namely, the return on my clients' investments. In fact, active funds typically carry expenses of 1.5 percent versus 0.5 percent for passive investing—a 1 percent difference that has a huge impact on investment returns.

For example, for a portfolio of $100,000 that yields 10 percent per year rather than 11 percent because of expenses, the difference is an extra $1,000 a year. (Compound that over 35 years, and you're talking about more than 1 million bucks!) Passive investing, I began to see, offered a singular advantage in terms of ultimate yield—an advantage, in sports terms, equivalent to starting on the 35-yard line in a football game versus on the 20; instead of having to get the ball 80 yards down the field for a touchdown, you have to move it only 65 yards—even less to get into field-goal range.

I Lose to a Brainless Index

My growing awareness of these realities was part and parcel of the more general realization dawning in my brain about money madness. The sheer stress of jumping from one fund to another had begun to get to me. My health had taken a back seat to the bottom line. I was exhausting myself, the returns I was realizing on investments were hardly exceptional, and I was paying a lot in expenses—that is, my clients were.

It seemed to me that I was pursuing an elusive goal and gaining mostly a lot of stress and sleepless nights. I began to feel a bit like the guy in the vegetable juice commercial who bops himself over the head in realization of his dumbness, except that, while the commercial is flippant, I was in a state of real dejection. There had to be a simpler, better way to get all those veggie vitamins—that is, to achieve the superior returns my clients deserved without the high costs to their bottom line and my health and well-being.

Certainly, the S&P 500 offered a simpler way. It was, therefore, something of a revelation to realize that the S&P 500 and the passive index funds that matched it were achieving better returns than all the active investing I was doing at enormous expense to my clients, my health, and my happiness.

At first, I fought the realization. I did not want to believe that some boring passive fund that absolutely anybody could invest in was smarter and more successful than Savvy Spencer. And in fact, my money monster worked overtime to get me to deny the realization. The reason? If it were true that a passive index fund of 500 stocks was more successful than I, with my Wharton MBA, my insight, and my determination, then I wasn't the powerhouse my money madness needed me to be. My shot at the cover of *Business Week* diminished with every point the S&P's performance exceeded my own. I was no longer the standout, the smartest boy in the class, the guy who had such control over money he could beat the market. Somewhere, way back in my mind, I was eight years old again, and a terrible sense of insecurity was flooding into my brain. If I couldn't do this money game as well as the S&P 500, who was I, and what was all my power and control worth?

Well, the facts were inescapable. For the years 1988 to 1992, if I had bought the index—invested in all 500 S&P stocks—I would have realized a 2.5 percent higher average return on my clients' investments than I actually achieved with all my frenzied active investing. So much for my late nights, sleeplessness, and exhaustion. So much for the adrenaline rush I had been chasing. So much for my money madness, which, in addition to making my life stressful and anxiety-ridden, wasn't even making me the big money.

It was not easy to give up on all this. In fact, it was just about the hardest thing I've ever had to do in my life—at least thus far. But the facts finally *could not* be denied: I couldn't beat the system, and believing that I could was dragging me and my life down; I simply had to let go.

I mean *really* let go: I stopped fighting my money monster. The belief that I had to outdo the market to be secure, the belief that had proven to be hollow time after time, simply evaporated.

I quit the adrenaline chase, relinquished the hell-bent pursuit of investment home runs, and gave up the active and reactive investing style I had long followed. Instead, I began to formulate the boring asset allocation strategy I would eventually call the Rainbow Portfolio. And once I did, a funny thing happened: More money came into my life. Much more money. In fact, I began to attract money like a magnet.

First, I invested solely in the S&P 500 and did better than I had done before—without a single gyration, just by staying put. Then, after a time, it occurred to me that the S&P, although offering stocks in a large number of different companies, was still, in a way, a single basket—large U.S. companies—in which to invest. So I began to *add* different kinds of investments to the S&P base, the idea being to participate in all sorts of market possibilities—still without any gyrations on my part, still just staying put with this wider portfolio of investments. And that's when the difference really began to show.

My clients noticed the difference, too. Certainly, they noticed that my new approach to their wealth left little opportunity for hitting the once-in-a-lifetime grand slam. But what they could not help but see was that they were doing better than ever. In fact, while the new strategy was a yawn to talk about, the return on investment it achieved was anything but humdrum. In fact, the returns my clients were now getting were nothing short of spectacular.

What was I doing to achieve these returns for my clients? Nothing. Almost literally. I was not watching the Dow and reacting to its slightest ratchet up or down. I was not reading the newspapers and shifting money from one asset class to another based on world events. I was not watching the talking heads on cable TV scream back and forth about stock picks, and I was not buying and selling as the pundits advised.

Where once my clients had seen me racing all over the place, reacting swiftly to every blip on the sonar of the global economy—so that it probably *looked like* I was working hard to make money for them— I was now out of that reactive loop. When a client asked me how the market was doing, I answered honestly that I did not know. I refrained from adding that I did not care, although, to my continuing embarrassment, I don't. (The embarrassment stems from a lingering notion that a person who makes his living in the investment advising business probably ought to care.)

Instead, thanks to the structure for achieving madness-free investing and staying there—the Rainbow Portfolio—I was earning more money on investments than I had ever thought possible, and I was beginning to feel the joy and richness of being bored to death by money.

What You'll Have to Give Up to Be Madness-Free

The cliché says that the sweetest fruit is at the top of the tree—up there where things are a little dangerous, up there where it's hard to get to. The strategy I structured as my Rainbow Portfolio is the low-hanging fruit, and we tend to look right past it. It's not as intriguing as the convoluted stratagems and calculations offered by all those other financial books and investment guides. It asks us to give up the chance, almost never realized, to pick an investment—a stock, a mutual fund, a real estate purchase—that will make us rich overnight. But the truth is, if that's a thrill you can't live without, buy a $1 lottery ticket and experience the same adrenaline rush—with almost as great a chance of winning.

The Rainbow Portfolio asks you to break your addiction to this adrenaline—a legal, widely available, seemingly free drug that feels very good pumping through our systems. It asks you to have faith that an alternative way of investing money—a boring way—will lead to more money, better sleep, higher energy levels, expanded time to pursue other life activities, and better health from the lowered adrenaline dosage coursing through your veins.

But the Rainbow Portfolio doesn't just ask you to relinquish all this; it enables you to do so by building it into the structure. The structure itself keeps me (and will keep you) from taking the temperature of the market at every moment and moving the needle up or down by millimeters to adjust a portfolio. Willpower is automatic. It's inherent in the structure.

So when your money monster shows up from time to time, as mine does, the structure allows for that. It lets the money monster prattle away—maybe tempting me to follow a friend's tip on an "investment that can't lose" or making me feel embarrassed that I don't know or care how the market is doing. The point is that no matter how great the temptation or how deep the embarrassment, the *structure* holds. Freedom from money madness is built in!

Yes, you may find that you can't join in the cocktail party chatter about the recession, or the exciting new start-up everyone else is pouring money into, or how now is the time to invest in wind power. But with *equity returns that have averaged at least 3 percent better than the S&P over the past 35 years*, that shouldn't be hard to give up. In fact, the Rainbow Portfolio realized an average return of 14 percent per year over the period, but relative return is a truer measure of investment success. Actually, relative to actively managed U.S. equity funds, the Rainbow Portfolio beat more than 96 percent of those funds over this period.

Where's the Rainbow—And
What's at the End of It?

Why do I call it the *Rainbow Portfolio?* It's not because there's a pot of gold at the end of this portfolio, although there most certainly is. No, the name derives from the super-diversification on which the portfolio is based, diversification that makes the portfolio look as colorful as a rainbow.

Diversification is central to sound and successful investing, and everybody knows it. Everybody knows the reason, too: Diversification spreads the risk of volatility, and volatility is what causes us to lose sleep at night and do something irrational where our investments are concerned. But the truth is, nobody knows for sure whether or when or by how much a portfolio will rise or fall in value.

I'm not saying there are no virtuosi in this business. Peter Lynch and Warren Buffett, to take perhaps the two best-known examples, do seem to have a kind of X-ray vision of the future; their predictions have proven singularly successful. But even they are not always right. Besides, such X-ray vision cannot be transferred and cannot be learned, as was demonstrated when Lynch personally trained his highly paid successors at Fidelity Investments—none of whom, since Lynch's departure, has been able to match his success. In fact, as a group, they were not even able to outperform the S&P.

Bottom line? The future is unsure.

What *is* pretty sure is that prices will fluctuate; we can also take it as a given that they will fluctuate differently at different times—that is, some stocks will go up while others go down in price. And then the ones that went down will go up, maybe even at the same time and by the same amount that the stocks that previously went up head down. But there's no certainty to any of this. The idea, therefore, is to diversify your portfolio so that when some stocks zig, others zag.

Why is this important? Think about farmers at the mercy of fluctuating weather that they cannot predict. As a hedge against the vagaries of weather—and as a way of trying to ensure they'll have some sort of harvest and some sort of income for the year—they plant a variety of crops in seasonal rotation. That way, if a drought wipes out the corn crop and a hurricane floods the wheat, there's still the apple orchard and the squash and the onions offering some hope of a harvestable crop come the autumn.

Similarly, if you invest in the 500 stocks of the S&P, you've invested in a great variety of companies and a great variety of stock price fluctuations. The variety as well as the number increase the probability that enough stocks will do sufficiently well to offset the negative performance of others and leave you ahead of the game, just as a good harvest of apples and squash and onions will compensate for the failed corn or wheat crop sufficiently to make you come out ahead for the year.

Diversifying with *Imperfect* Correlation

The technical term for this kind of reciprocal relationship is *correlation*, and what you want ideally in a portfolio is a range of investments that are in *imperfect correlation* to one another. The reason is simple: Companies that are well correlated tend to behave similarly as investments; they tend to respond the same to a particular economic event.

If you invest in both Giant Airlines and Humongous Airlines, for example, you are investing in two similar, large companies in the same industry. Chances are when the stock of one goes up, so does the stock of the other. Or suppose you own two Manhattan apartments; one may be in a high-rise with a view and the other a cozy brownstone "floor-through" with a garden. But they're both still Manhattan apartments, so if the bottom falls out of the Manhattan real estate market, the value of both apartments is likely to tank.

But suppose you buy stock in Giant Airlines and County Airlines, a local start-up run by a friend of yours. If oil prices spike and County goes under, chances are pretty good that Giant will still be flying— and you won't lose everything. And if your second apartment is in Tulsa, Oklahoma, and not in that high-rise on the classy East Side of Manhattan, a downturn in the New York real estate market may well fail to ripple as far outward as the Sooner State. Again, you won't lose all you have.

So it turns out that while there is no particular advantage to investing your money in things that behave similarly, there *is* a particular advantage to investing in things that behave even slightly differently—a hedging-your-bet advantage at the least and a maximizing-your-gain advantage at best.

Think in Terms of Asset Class

The driving force in this behavior is asset class. An asset class is simply a group of investments that tend to respond to economic events in a similar way. Large companies, regardless of their industry, tend to respond similarly to one another and differently from small companies. The stock price of a small community bank is more closely correlated to that of a small paper-clip manufacturer than to that of a large bank. The reason? The small bank and small manufacturer do completely different things, but they share an asset class—small value stocks—and it is asset class, not industry, that determines performance.

Around the turn of the millennium, studies by scholars like Charles Ellis, a Yale economist, began to demonstrate conclusively what I had long intuited and still believe: that it is asset class that really drives return on investment, not individual stocks, not company performance, not a company's underlying fundamentals or its quarterly statement. Ellis's studies showed in fact that on average only 4 percent of a stock price's movement could be explained as deriving from its performance; 96 percent derived from the asset class the company belonged to.[2]

The S&P index represents 500 different companies, but it really covers only one asset class—that of large market-capitalization (large-cap) U.S. companies. That is why in the two years 1973 to 1974 and again from 2000 to 2002, the S&P dropped 37 percent and 38 percent, respectively—the worst declines for the S&P apart from the Great Depression. Because almost everything in the index was in the same asset class, it pretty much all behaved the same.

Asset class was the key, I concluded, and diversification needed to be on the basis of asset class, not company. The more asset classes in the portfolio, the less correlation there would be. The less correlation, the less volatility. The less volatility, the greater the chance for avoiding loss and thereby achieving gain.

As I saw it, investing in the S&P 500 was like playing baseball with a team of nine pitchers. Even though all the pitchers were pretty good, they were really good only at pitching, and I wanted instead to field a whole team of skills—a portfolio of varied talents, attributes, and capabilities.

The Eighth Wonder of the World

But there's even more to it than that. One of your goals in investing is to gain access to the magic of compounding, which no less an authority than Albert Einstein is said to have dubbed "the eighth wonder of the world."

Einstein's approval may be myth—or wishful thinking—but compounding is powerful stuff. Simply put, it means generating earnings from previous earnings.

If you buy a stock for $100, and it rises in value 10 percent for the year, you earn $10 and end up with a total of $110. If the stock goes up 10 percent again the following year, you earn $11—10 percent of your previously earned $110—so your original $100 has now grown to $121! That's compounding.

The real magic comes when you combine the growth benefit of compounding with the decreased volatility of investing in multiple, imperfectly correlated stocks. Take Steve. A savvy investor, he put $100 into Smith Corporation, a large-cap U.S. company, and another $100 into Chang Corporation, a small international company. Sure enough, over a three-year period, the Smith stock zigged while that of Chang zagged. But because Steve was invested in both, one stock offset the other, and the volatility of this zigging and zagging was neutralized. The result, despite some wild jumps—Chang up 45 percent one year, Smith down 25 percent another year—was a steady 10 percent average return.

The magic came from compounding that smoothly consistent yield year after year after year. By contrast, if Steve had put the whole $200 in Smith or Chang alone, he would have been compounding erratic returns instead of the steady 10 percent annual return. Compounded over 30 years at 10 percent, Steve's $200 in the two stocks will grow to $3,490—versus $1,716 at most if he had invested in just one. That's the magic: more than twice as much money.

	Smith Corp: Annual Return	Chang Corp: Annual Return	Smith + Chang: Annual Return (Smith return + Chang return divided by 2)
Year 1	−25%	+45%	10%
Year 2	+30%	−10%	10%
Year 3	+25%	−5%	10%
Average	10%	10%	10%

Add it up: Consistency of return through diversifying on the basis of imperfect correlation *plus* compounding equals more money.

All the Colors of the Spectrum

Now I'm not the only person to have figured this out. The benefits of diversification are hardly my personal secret. Indeed, to achieve these benefits for their clients, fund managers, brokers, and bank trust managers routinely boast that they invest their clients' money in as many as four key asset classes. Here's a typical allocation:

- Bonds: 25 percent
- Large value stocks: 20 percent
- Large U.S. growth stocks: 40 percent
- Large international stocks: 15 percent

Indeed, the typical investment portfolio even today is allocated just this way—in these four different shades, so to speak, of investing, represented in the pie chart below.

Typical Investment Portfolio Allocation

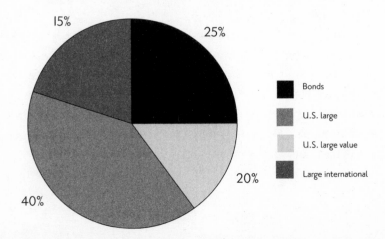

But I had a different idea. I wanted to take diversification to a whole new level—both to minimize volatility and to take advantage of the faster, bigger growth that could come through compounding. So I began searching for more and more asset classes—more and more colors—until I finally came up with 14, the double rainbow, represented as the pie chart below.

The Rainbow Portfolio

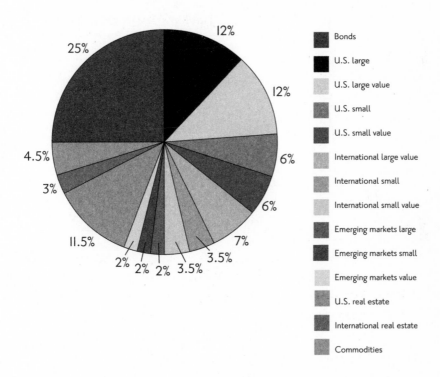

Legend:
- Bonds
- U.S. large
- U.S. large value
- U.S. small
- U.S. small value
- International large value
- International small
- International small value
- Emerging markets large
- Emerging markets small
- Emerging markets value
- U.S. real estate
- International real estate
- Commodities

Chart percentages: 12%, 12%, 6%, 6%, 7%, 3.5%, 3.5%, 2%, 2%, 2%, 11.5%, 3%, 4.5%, 25%

It is an unusual level of asset class diversity—at least 10 more asset classes than most portfolios contain. But this isn't just a matter of quantity. Each asset within the Rainbow Portfolio brings the benefit of being imperfectly correlated with the other asset classes in the portfolio. And each such addition thereby ratchets up the potential for decreasing volatility and making you more money—on average at least 3 percent better than the S&P.

Fortunately, there are mutual funds dedicated to each of these asset classes that are available to individual investors, and you can create your own Rainbow Portfolio by investing in a range of these funds.* You thus get the benefits of the Rainbow Portfolio's diversity without having to buy individual stocks to compose each asset class on your own. Some funds representing each asset class are given in the table below.

Funds Available in Rainbow Portfolio Asset Classes**

Asset Class	Fund	Symbol
Bonds (For low-tax-bracket investors or tax-deferred accounts)	Vanguard Total Bond Market Index	VBMFX
Bonds (For high-tax-bracket investors in taxable accounts)	Vanguard Intermediate Term Tax-Exempt	VWITX
U.S. large	Fidelity Spartan 500 Index Investor	FSMKX
	iShares S&P 500 Index (ETF)	IVV
U.S. large value	Vanguard Value Index	VIVAX
	iShares Russell 3000 Value Index (ETF)	IWW
U.S. small	Vanguard Small-Cap Index	NAESX
	iShares Russell 2000 Index (ETF)	IWM

*The funds that I recommend most highly are those from Dimensional Fund Advisors, which are available only through financial advisors. See www.curemoneymadness.com for more information.

**Available at the time of writing.

Asset Class	Fund	Symbol
U.S. small value	Vanguard Small-Cap Value Index	VISVX
	iShares Russell 2000 Value Index (ETF)	IWN
International large value	Fidelity Spartan International Index Investor	FSIIX
	iShares MSCI EAFE Value Index (ETF)	EFV
International small value	SPDR S&P International Small Cap (ETF)	GWX
International small	Vanguard International Explorer	VINEX
	iShares MSCI EAFE Small Cap Index	SCZ
Emerging markets large	Vanguard Emerging Markets Stock Index	VEIEX
	iShares MSCI Emerging Markets Index (ETF)	EEM
Emerging markets small	WisdomTree Emerging Markets Small Cap Dividend Fund	DGS
Emerging markets value	Schwab Fundamental Emerging Markets Index	SFENX
	WisdomTree Emerging Markets High (ETF)	DEM
U.S. real estate	Vanguard REIT Index	VGSIX
	SPDR DJ Wilshire REIT (ETF)	RWR

Asset Class	Fund	Symbol
International real estate	Fidelity International Real Estate	FIREX
	SPDR D| Wilshire International Real Estate	RWX
Commodities	PIMCO Commodity Real Return Strat D	PCRDX
	ELEMENTS Rogers International Commodity Total Return	R|I

You don't just make more with the Rainbow Portfolio, you keep more. Diversification and imperfect correlation provide protection for your investments when times are bad and markets in general head downward. The first year for which we have statistics on all the asset classes within the Rainbow Portfolio is 1973, and in the period 1973–74, when the S&P lost 37 percent, the Rainbow Portfolio was down only 27 percent. In 2000–02, when the S&P lost 38 percent, the Rainbow Portfolio lost a mere 0.6 percent; it basically held steady. Over the period 1973–2007, the S&P had eight negative years, the Rainbow Portfolio only five.

In other words, the Rainbow Portfolio has fewer down years than even the classic passive investing embodied in the S&P 500 index, and in the years when the Rainbow Portfolio too is down, it is down by less, often far less. And of course, when it is up—and it is mostly up: 86 percent of the time since it was started, in fact—its 14 percent average return is more up than that of the S&P 500, which averaged an 11 percent return over the same period.

Bottom line? Diversification is good, and more diversification—carefully and deliberately applied—is better, as the Rainbow Portfolio's results make clear. See for yourself by examining the following graph.

Rainbow Portfolio performance compared to S&P 500 and average U.S. Large-Cap Mutual Fund for $10,000 invested January 1, 1973, through December 31, 2007

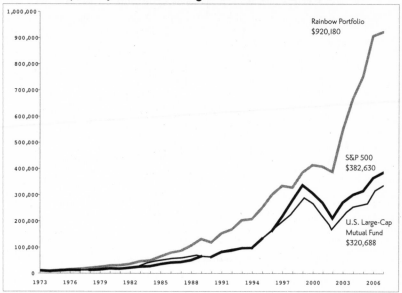

The Winning Formula Known as "Small-and-Boring"

There's another essential component that distinguishes the Rainbow Portfolio. It's the inclusion in a highly focused way of the small value asset class, comprising smaller companies whose stock is underpriced. (In Wall Street terms, value stocks have a low price-to-book or price-to-earnings or price-to-sales ratio.) I like to think of this asset class as the small-and-boring asset class, and it's key to the Rainbow Portfolio for one very simple reason: More money can be made by investing in these smaller, boring companies than in the big, exciting, high-growth companies that tend to steal the headlines.

Why smaller companies? Almost by definition they're riskier and more volatile than larger companies. After all, large companies got large by doing well; they're proven commodities. Smaller companies haven't yet demonstrated their worth or their staying power; statistically, small businesses are far more likely to go out of business than large ones. But precisely because of their riskiness, smaller companies offer the potential of a higher rate of growth. You invest in Joe's Cars rather than in Ford or Toyota because, if Joe's succeeds, it will pay a lot more, and it will pay it faster. Historically, in fact, when small, volatile, risky companies like a Joe's Cars do well, they do very well. So smallness, with its potentially high returns, is something the Rainbow Portfolio looks for.

The other favorable component is that a company be boring. By *boring* I mean less visible to investors, not featured on the high-decibel TV shows or written up in analysts' reports or purchased like the latest fashions by people in the know who always have the latest everything. Boring means General Mills, not Google—to take one example—that is, boring old breakfast cereal, not a history-making, planet-conquering, on-everybody's-lips Internet search engine. Stocks that are boring in the General Mills way are just simply cheaper than exciting Google-like stocks; you're paying less for the same level of profits. And, ironically, over the years, these boring companies have consistently performed much better than large and exciting companies.

To see this illustrated, go back 35-plus years, to a time when the General Mills vs. Google investing choice might have been between Proctor & Gamble (P&G) and IBM—between soap and the System 360, at the time the most exciting innovation imaginable. IBM certainly grew much faster and more spectacularly than did staid Proctor & Gamble. Back then, however, with expectations for IBM similar to the speedy growth expectations for Google today, IBM's stock price was inflated. In other words, you paid more for every dollar of profit IBM earned than for P&G's profits.

In fact, given the high price of IBM and given also that P&G over time cut its costs significantly through the efficiencies of new technologies, P&G actually turned out to be much the better bet as an investment despite IBM's higher growth rate of earnings.

How high? For the period 1970–2006, the stock price of IBM appreciated at the rate of 8.9 percent per year; the stock price of P&G appreciated at the rate of 15.5 percent per year. It means that while $10,000 invested in IBM in 1970 would be worth some $215,000 today, the same amount invested in P&G would be worth $1.7 million.

That's why the Rainbow Portfolio's diversification includes companies that are boring like Proctor & Gamble or General Mills *and* small like a Joe's Cars. The combination is an exceptional formula for minimizing risk while still achieving high returns.

Small-and-Boring Returns Can Be Big and Exciting

Here's a look at how a one-time investment of $1,000 in 1927 in six different asset classes would have accumulated in terms of both amount and annual rate of return. I choose 1927 because it's the first year for which figures on all these asset classes are available. The irony is that most investors today have the bulk of their money in large growth stocks, which, as the chart below clearly shows, have offered the worst relative returns.

Asset Class	Earnings on $1,000 Invested January 1927 (as of December 2007)	Annual Rate of Return
Large growth	$1,446,782	9.4%
Large U.S. (S&P 500)	2,809,419	10.3%
Large value	5,426,100	11.2%
Small growth	1,343,486	9.3%
Small	11,205,246	12.2%
Small value (small and boring)	40,671,759	14.0%

Value stocks beat growth stocks, small beats big, and small value—that is, small and boring—tops the charts. In other words, if your grandparents had had $1,000 to invest on your behalf in 1927 and had put it in small-and-boring value stocks, you'd be sitting pretty today. Boring the companies may be: When you tell your fellow guests at a dinner party that one of the numerous asset classes you invest in consists of small, dull companies no one has ever heard of and someone else says he has just bought stock in wind farms, heads around the table are going to swing his way, not yours. At least until people look at the numbers: $40 million from investing in small and boring versus $2.8 million from the S&P 500. That's pretty compelling.

That's why the focus on small and boring is a key distinguishing factor of the Rainbow Portfolio; it's the sleeper asset class that delivers the surprise punch for the portfolio.

Bearing Witness—Passively

"So okay," you may be saying to yourself right about now. "I want the returns the Rainbow Portfolio promises, and I'm ready to do whatever it takes to get those returns. Where do I sign up?"

Well, the harsh reality is that signing up isn't enough. You also have to just sit there. You have to stop keeping score. You have to stop trying to predict the future. You have to stop getting hysterical and ordering your broker to "Sell!" when one piece of your particular Rainbow Portfolio pie gets smaller; in fact, you actually have to let him or her buy more of that slice.

I call it witness discipline. It's what I've learned to do when the weather turns warm in March and thoughts of tomatoes enter my mind: I savor the warmth and go back inside the house. I do not go to the garage and hunt around for the hoe and the spade. I do not order seeds. I witness my pleasure in the warm temperatures and my excitement about the tomatoes I'll start growing in a few months—and then I put it all out of my mind.

Witness discipline investing is a built-in feature of the Rainbow Portfolio. It's also an essential element of the cure for money madness and an important strategic component of madness-free investing. Here's the reason: Doing anything other than witnessing gets you nowhere. It doesn't work. It's an expenditure of effort that is frequently exasperating and almost always exhausting. And 95 times out of 100 you will actually make less money.

You don't have to take my word for it; listen to the experts:

In 2004, a reporter from Minnesota, Jeff Brown of TwinCities.com, decided to write an article on money managers, the people who choose and monitor the investments in individual investor portfolios.[3] To write his piece, the reporter quite naturally turned to Morningstar, the leading research and rating firm on mutual funds, and asked to look at the performance records of large-cap funds—that is, active funds invested in the same asset class as the S&P 500. Morningstar told the reporter there were 1,446 such funds, and they determined that over the 10-year period ending in October 2004, only 35 *out of the 1,446* matched or beat the performance of the index.

As Brown quickly determined, 35 "winners" out of 1,446 meant that exactly **2.4 percent of money managers did better than the S&P 500 index, for all their research and fund-shifting and asset reallocation and late nights at the office,** and the percentage pretty much went to zero if you factored in taxes.

What does this tell us? It's confirmation, if more were needed, that passive investing—not stock picking, not looking for mispriced securities, not actively managing a fund, but just passively bearing witness to an index-mirroring portfolio—realizes superior returns for far less effort and virtually no stress. It tells us to go back in the house; tomatoes get planted in May.

And it's a message to recap the basics of the Rainbow Portfolio:

1. Invest in a distinctively high number of asset classes—
    14, at current count. (This *could* change; check my
    website at www.curemoneymadness.com for updates.)
2. Emphasize small and boring.
3. Practice witness discipline.

With all that in mind, are you ready to create your own Rainbow Portfolio? Doing so will require you to make one basic decision first, then to create your own allocation formula, and then, once a year, to undertake a pretty simple rebalancing that works almost automatically.

Unless you're good at keeping a lot of numbers jumping around in your head at one time, you might want to grab a pencil and a piece of paper for this.

Part I
The Bond Decision

The first step toward creating your personal Rainbow Portfolio is to allocate your total investment assets to particular asset classes on paper. And your first decision is the bond decision: determining how much of your portfolio should be in corporate or government bonds and how much in the equities that make up the other 13 asset classes. (I invest in high-quality government and corporate bond index funds only; junk bonds are out!) Figuring out that basic two-part split will fundamentally affect the amount of money you make from your investments. Here's why.

As I constantly tell participants in my workshops, for all the myriad investment products available, there are still only two basic ways to invest: You either lend money to a company or real estate project or you own a piece of the company or the property. That is, you're either a bondholder (lender) or a stockholder/equity holder (owner).

If you're an equity holder who participates in owning a company or property, you're an insider who shares the rewards but also the risks of ownership. You could win big, but you could also lose—a little, a lot, or everything.

By contrast, if you lend money as a bondholder, you can't expect terrifically high rewards, but you also needn't lie awake nights worrying about risk. With bonds—whether issued by a corporation, municipality, or the federal government—the full face value of the bond is backed up by the issuer, plus you receive a guaranteed interest payment. Unless the corporation or municipality or the federal government goes bankrupt, you'll get your money back.

Bonds protect you in troubled times and hurt you in boom years. For example, in the 1973–74 market downturn, a Rainbow Portfolio with zero bonds decreased in value by 27 percent, while one that had 60 percent in bonds decreased by only 2 percent. (The same thing happened with the S&P 500, only the decreases were much larger: 37

percent down with zero bonds, and a decrease of 15 percent in value with 60 percent bonds.) In the correction of 2000–02, a Rainbow Portfolio with zero percent in bonds decreased in value by less than 1 percent, while one that had 60 percent in bonds gained 13 percent. During the Great Depression (when not all the Rainbow Portfolio asset classes even existed), the S&P 500 all-equity portfolio *lost 8.6 percent* during the 10-year period 1929–38, while a portfolio of 60 percent government bonds and 40 percent S&P 500 actually *gained 43 percent* over the same period. Bottom line: Bonds protect you in the most troubled times.

That's simply the nature of bond behavior. While owning bonds is the surest way to decrease volatility in a portfolio, there's a limit to how far you can go. In fact, when too big a percentage of the portfolio is in bonds—more than 80 percent, for example—the bonds both decrease your returns and, ironically, increase volatility.

That's why I think of bonds as similar to putting training wheels on the motorcycle of the Rainbow Portfolio; they offer stability, reduce volatility, and let you sleep better at night, but they also slow down the engine of return on investment.

So the key driver of your Rainbow Portfolio is to determine how much stability versus volatility is right for you given your investment goals. Where's your balance point between bonds and equities, the place where you feel comfortable that you're both achieving sufficient returns and sleeping at night?

The chart on p. 144 will help you find that point. Whatever you're investing for—whether retirement or to pay for your daughter's wedding or to roam the world for a certain number of years—there are two metrics for determining how much of your portfolio to allocate to bonds:

1. The number of years before you're going to start withdrawing money from the portfolio for this goal.
2. The number of years over which money is to be withdrawn.

Take a look.

Finding Your Portfolio's Bond Allocation

		Number of years over which money is to be withdrawn								
		0	**5**	**10**	**15**	**20**	**25**	**30**	**35**	**40**
	1	100	65	60	55	50	45	40	35	30
	2	80	60	55	50	45	35	35	30	25
Number	**5**	70	55	50	45	40	35	30	25	20
of years	**10**	40	35	30	25	20	15	10	5	0
before	**15**	30	25	20	15	10	0	0	0	0
withdrawal	**20**	25	20	15	10	5	0	0	0	0
of money	**25**	20	15	10	5	0	0	0	0	0
begins	**30**	15	10	5	0	0	0	0	0	0
	35	10	5	0	0	0	0	0	0	0
	40	5	0	0	0	0	0	0	0	0

Percentage points to add to your result to adjust for concern over volatility: If you check the market daily, add 20 percentage points; if you check the market weekly, add 10 percentage points; and if you check the market monthly, add 5 percentage points. If you don't check the market at all, no additions are necessary.

Down the vertical axis, find the number of years before you want to start withdrawing funds. Across the horizontal axis, identify the number of years over which you plan to withdraw the funds. Where the two meet is the percentage of your portfolio you should be allocating to bonds.

For example, if you're investing in order to have a lump sum of cash to pay for your daughter's wedding a year from now—that is, a once-only withdrawal one year away—you want 100 percent of your portfolio in bonds. If your dream is to spend 5 years drifting around the globe 10 years from now, that's 5 years of withdrawals on the horizontal axis and 10 years before you start withdrawing on the vertical axis. Answer: You want 35 percent of your portfolio allocated to bonds.

Certainly, not every goal falls neatly into 5-year increments, so you'll want to adjust up or down if either your withdrawal date or withdrawal period is 17 years or 22 years or the like. Use your judgment: Round up the number of years if you want to be more aggressive, round down to take a more conservative stance.

Note that you'll also have to adjust your bond allocation percentage to account for your money madness. If you suffer from the kind of high-level money madness that drives you to check the market daily, you clearly have a greater need for the stability of training wheels; it means you need to allocate more of your portfolio to bonds than does someone less governed by emotion. So if you're one of those people who needs to see how your stocks are doing every day, add 20 points to the percentage of your portfolio allocated to bonds. If you check the market only weekly, add 10 points. Monthly checkers need add only 5 percentage points. Only folks who don't check the market get off without paying a penalty for their money madness.

Also, you may have a number of different investment goals—your daughter's wedding *and* your 5-year world tour *and* retirement. So think in terms of a different portfolio for each, and determine separate and distinct bond allocations for each.

Most portfolios, to be sure, will end up allocating less to bonds and more to equities. After all, with the Rainbow Portfolio, the level of diversification among equities is sufficient to decrease risk even as you decrease your bond allocation. That's the strength of the Rainbow Portfolio. It's also in line with the core message of this book: Our fear—in this case, our fear of stock market volatility—is a product of money madness, not a reflection of reality.

And speaking of reality, it's advisable to redo this training wheels calculation once every 5 years to keep your bond decision up to date.

Part 2
Allocate

Once you've determined the percentage you'll allocate to bonds, you're ready to grab a calculator and color in your portfolio pie chart.

First, as you've just done, find your portfolio's bond allocation and subtract that percentage from 100 percent. The remainder is what I call the REA percentage: the Rainbow Equities Allocation. For example, if your portfolio's bond allocation is 20 percent, that leaves 80 percent for equities; that's your REA. Write yours down.

My REA

In the REA table below I list the percentages of your total assets I recommend you allocate to each non-bond asset class of your Rainbow Portfolio. To determine *your* equity percentages, multiply by *your* REA percentage.

The Rainbow Portfolio Allocation

Asset Class	REA Percentage
U.S. real estate	15% x my REA =
International real estate	4% x my REA =
Commodities (gold, silver, oil, gas, etc.)	6% x my REA =
U.S. large*	16% x my REA =

Asset Class	REA Percentage
U.S. large value**	16% x my REA =
U.S. small*	8% x my REA =
U.S. small value**	8% x my REA =
International large value**	9% x my REA =
International small*	4.5% x my REA =
International small value**	4.5% x my REA =
Emerging markets large*	3% x my REA =
Emerging markets small*	3% x my REA =
Emerging markets value**	3% x my REA =
Your Rainbow Portfolio bond allocation	
Total	100%

Please note that the real estate asset class does not include the equity in your home, if you own your own home—and that includes a second or vacation home. Your home is where you live, and if you have a second home, that's also where you live; presumably, you bought it to live in. But if you own a rental property, include the equity value; it's an investment.

Of course, nothing is static—especially when it comes to money, the economy, and the financial markets. As I continue to learn more about money, and as the global economy shifts, I might change a percentage in the formula, add an asset class, or delete an asset class. To stay current, visit my website at www.curemoneymadness.com. There, the Rainbow Portfolio allocation prescription will always be up to date.

*These blended funds contain a combination of both growth and value stocks.

**These funds have an even deeper value orientation and have lower price-to-book, price-to-sale, or price-to-earnings ratios than the value stocks contained in the blended funds.

Rebalance. Period.

Isn't there anything at all to *do* once you have invested in the Rainbow Portfolio? Isn't there some action that can be taken? Well, yes. The Rainbow Portfolio strategy calls for annual rebalancing of the portfolio so that it doesn't get too top heavy in some asset classes and too meager in others. I recommend setting a date for this recurring appointment; January is my preferred time. In addition, if the market takes a real dive or hits a real high, you might want to take another look before your annual rebalancing anniversary.

The rebalancing process is like deflating car tires that are overinflated and inflating tires that are losing air—and it's equally simple. For example, if you begin with a 40:60 bond-to-equities ratio for your portfolio, and a year later, on your rebalancing anniversary, you find that bonds have deflated to 30 percent while equities are up to 70 percent of your total portfolio, you've got some rebalancing to do. You need to sell enough of the funds in the asset classes that have spiked to get back to your original prescription, and use the proceeds to buy more bonds. This will bring you back to the 40:60 bond-to-equities allocation that you determined was right for you.

The beauty of rebalancing is that it forces you to do something that is emotionally difficult: buy low and sell high. It's a tool for automatically getting you back to your original Rainbow Portfolio allocation—a built-in money monster avoidance mechanism.

Again, check out the website at www.curemoneymadness.com for computer help with all of this.

The Rainbow Portfolio and Your Employer-Sponsored Retirement Plan

If you're like more and more Americans, you're probably enrolled in the employer-sponsored retirement plan known as a 401(k) if you work in a for-profit corporation; a 403(b) in the nonprofit universe; and a 457 plan or other variant if you work for local, state, or the federal government.

If so, good for you! The advantages of these employer-sponsored retirement plans are pretty amazing; I tell my clients that if they do the math, they'll see that these plans are the most underrated gift in human history! All are tax-deferred, meaning you won't pay any taxes on either your contributions to the plan or your earnings from it until you actually withdraw the money. As if that weren't enough of an incentive to invest in these plans, many employers match some or all of every employee's contribution—in some cases actually doubling what you put in. That's like free money. And for those who find it hard to keep track of such things, most plans also offer an automatic contribution mechanism, so the amount you choose to invest is automatically deducted from your paycheck and directed into your investment account.

In other words, these plans make it both attractive and easy to save and invest money for retirement. Under the circumstances, you'd think corporate employees would be chomping at the bit to sign up.

You'd be wrong. In a pervasive kind of money madness, **30 percent of workers eligible for retirement plans don't bother to participate. And 70 percent of those who do participate invest primarily—some almost exclusively—in their company's stock, despite such dramatic disasters as Enron and Bear Stearns, in which many employees who were invested in the company stock lost it all. And nearly half of participants don't contribute enough to get the full company match, which is like saying no to free money.**

We all know that Americans are notorious for not saving—even when these 401(k) plans make it easy. At the high end of the earning scale, perhaps the indifference is part of that old money madness idea that you can beat your company-sponsored retirement plan by managing your own investments. Since investing on your own sets you against the headwind of taxes, that's hard to do; if the company plan returns 10 percent, you'd have to realize at least 12 percent to do better. Among people living paycheck to paycheck, the madness is that when you get a raise, you raise your spending as well—and live paycheck to paycheck at a higher income, still not saving.

Either way, given the tax deferment and, where offered, the incentive of employer-matched contributions, it is madness to disdain these plans. Even a Warren Buffett would not have beaten a 401(k) with a matching contribution from the employer—especially if the match were substantive. That's why I recommend doing just about whatever you have to do to invest in these plans. If you find it difficult to save, start small. Do the minimum contribution possible at first, then ask your employer to increase it over time. If you feel strapped for cash, take some out of other savings to take advantage of a 401(k) plan with a match. In certain situations, I've even recommended that a client take out a loan to fund participation in his company's 401(k) with a match. It's that good an investment vehicle.

And as much as possible, your aim should be to make your 401(k) an essential part of your overall personal Rainbow Portfolio. Most 401(k)s won't be able to offer the Rainbow Portfolio's 14 asset classes, but you can still use other resources, if available, to invest on your own to complement your 401(k).

The first thing to do is to check the investment options available in your employer's retirement plan. Most offer a menu of funds, which, to comply with Department of Labor standards, run the gamut of risk from conservative to aggressive and everything in between. Yet as far as asset class diversification is concerned, employer-sponsored retirement plans pretty much limit themselves to the four standards: large-cap U.S. growth, large-cap U.S. value, large international growth, and bonds or fixed income. To find out which asset classes are available in your employer's menu of funds, you can look at each fund's literature, which is usually offered online or can be mailed to you at your request. In addition, there are mutual fund rating services, like Morningstar, that categorize virtually all funds by asset class.

Keep in mind that it's possible for a fund to represent more than one asset class. For example, if ABC Mutual Fund is 75 percent invested in U.S. large growth stocks and 25 percent in international large growth, you'll need to be aware that that's how your money is allocated; in a sense, you're "catching" two asset classes with one fund. In any event, once you find out which asset class or classes your employer's plan gives you access to, you at least know where you are— and where and how far you need to go to reach the 14-asset-class mark of the Rainbow Portfolio.

The next step is to add whichever of the 14 asset classes you cannot get through your employer plan, using a financial advisor or by do-it-yourself mutual fund investing. For example, if your employer-sponsored plan offers funds that invest only in domestic equities, buy your international equities on your own. Keep adding outside asset classes till you make up the 14-asset-class portfolio on your own, or come as close as you can. That way, you reap the advantages of your employer-sponsored plan—the tax deferment, the matching funds, the convenience—and the gains of the Rainbow Portfolio.

Another easy way to gain such advantages is to roll over retirement plans from previous employers into an IRA rollover account where you can take advantage of the increased number of asset class offerings to supplement your current 401(k). The ultimate goal here too, of course, is a total portfolio that profiles the 14 asset classes of the Rainbow Portfolio.

As to investing in your company stock, don't. You're already subject to the risks and rewards of your company's future through your employment there; in a very real sense, you're already correlated to its performance. Why invest in its stock as well? It shocks me to learn that 42 percent of total 401(k) assets are invested in the company's stock; your aim should be zero percent of your 401(k) in the company's stock. Of course, if you can buy your company's stock at a discount, buying it and selling it quickly may offer you a gain that you can then diversify into investments representing varied asset classes—a full rainbow of them. But if participating in your employer-sponsored retirement plan is all you can afford, just try to make that plan as close to the Rainbow Portfolio as possible.

Don't forget that as an employee, you can potentially help expand your company's retirement plan offering. You do have a say in the matter. The Investment Company Institute of Washington, D.C., estimates that as of the end of 2006, some 80 million of us were enrolled in such plans, representing investments totaling more than $4.1 trillion. Those numbers ought to constitute a pretty good-size bullhorn. And as it happens, now is a particularly good time to advocate for bringing the benefits of the Rainbow Portfolio to your organization's plan. The reason is that plan sponsors—that is, employers who set up retirement plans—are under increasing pressure to answer for the plans in terms of risk and performance. Lawsuits have been brought charging that certain plan sponsors didn't keep the fees reasonable enough.[4] One result is that plan sponsors are more interested than ever in making sure employees are happy with the plans.

So, as I noted, now may be a good time to try to inspire your employer to offer funds that cover as many of the 14 asset classes of the Rainbow Portfolio as possible and that manage those investments passively. With employers in a persuadable frame of mind, you might just want to remind them that making more money with less volatility—through a greater number of asset classes, not just fund choices, and through passive investing, not frenzied active management—can lead to less financially stressed employees, higher plan participation, and greater retention of valuable employees, all of which sponsors want.

If you're self-employed or your employer doesn't offer a retirement plan, do the same thing: Mimic the 14 asset classes of the Rainbow Portfolio in your retirement and non-retirement accounts.

What's the Difference?

For many employees, an employer-sponsored plan represents their total retirement nest egg. If you're 35 years old today and are enrolled in an employer-sponsored retirement plan, investing in 14 asset classes as opposed to the four standard asset classes of most 401(k)s could make an 80 percent difference in the size of your portfolio when you reach age 65. Applying the average index returns from 1973 to 2007, for example, the four asset classes would yield $1 million in retirement assets, while a Rainbow Portfolio with the same bond allocation would yield $1.8 million. Over the 30-year period, you'd earn even less than the lower figure—half a million less—if the four asset classes were actively managed, as employer-sponsored retirement plans tend to be.

Bottom line: More asset classes are better, passive management is better, and the Rainbow Portfolio does it all for you. It's madness-free investing. All it asks is that you keep your emotions away from your portfolio.

CHAPTER 7

Getting Money

Madness-Free Strategies

Whether rich or poor, we spend considerable time, effort, and energy getting money. But we get money more effectively and less stressfully—and we actually get more money—when we go after it cured of our money madness.

Most of us work for a living, and to a great extent, our work lives are ruled by the money madness planted in us when we were children. Mine was. No matter what I earned, it was never enough, and finding out that a colleague made a higher salary would send me into a tailspin—of panic, envy, anger, and anxiety. I didn't consider the value I was producing for my company or my job level, or whether I was being fairly compensated or not, or even how the economy was faring. I just saw myself in relation to the colleague who was making *more*, the colleague who was winning while I was losing and who was therefore a threat to my security fortress. If I were buying a sound system for the house, I would rationally compare prices of all the components at different stores, compiling the data conscientiously. But I never looked at whether I was underpaid, overpaid, or fairly paid in terms of the prevailing compensation for my colleagues and competitors. By keeping the blinders on, my money monster had a field day assuring me I was never making enough money, no matter what.

Mine isn't the only way money madness sabotages our work lives. I have a friend, Lucy, who tossed off her résumé in a couple of hours one Sunday night before a job interview. It looked it. It had typos, grammatical errors, and formatting inconsistencies, was intimidating to read, and, once read, was unpersuasive. Yet it's well known that a good résumé opens doors—maybe to a job that in total compensation could be worth millions of dollars over the next 10 to 30 years. In being so cavalier about that tool, Lucy was not just sabotaging her chances for the job, she was also setting up a good excuse for not getting it. That was Lucy's money madness: Money Hatred, one of the top 10 money behaviors defined in Chapter 1, and fear of making a lot of it.

Then there's Bruce. He had two job offers last week, and it was no contest: He went for the higher starting salary. Yet even a little bit of probing revealed that the longer commute the higher-paying job required—and the attendant higher commuting costs—virtually wiped out the salary differential between the two offers. Moreover, a simple question about average salary increases at the two companies made it clear that the job with the lower starting salary offered higher salary increases—and offered them sooner. Bruce blew it. All his money madness could see was the higher dollar figure right now; it wasn't the whole picture—not even close. You won't be surprised to hear that Bruce doesn't have a clue how much he spends or what his net worth is, either. He doesn't want to know the details of his money situation; he's a classic case of Taking a Siesta, another of the top 10.

We've seen how money madness can blind us to the facts when it comes to investing and can insulate us inside our personal relationships. It can have a similar effect on our work life, obscuring the realities of compensation over a lifetime, of the importance of a résumé, and of the ancillary costs and benefits of a job. And we pay the price for this blindness in stress, anxiety, confusion, discomfort, less than effective performance on the job, and far less joy and fulfillment in the work that consumes so much of our lives.

Lose the madness, however, and what's left is the work itself—shorn of its power to engage your emotions about money and thus free from being ruled by them. Get your money monster to heel, shift your focus from your fears and fantasies to the financial facts, and you gain a happier, more fulfilling outcome—better job performance, a less stressful and more rewarding work life, and a fatter wallet as well.

So in this chapter, I'll offer strategies for approaching work in a madness-free way and for two activities that I view as being intrinsically bound up with getting money—selling and asking for money. In a sense, everything we do at work is about selling; all day long, we're selling *ourselves*, putting our performance on the line. Every presentation by a corporate manager, every trim and style a hairdresser does, every truck ride hauling a load of freight from Boston to Boise is a sales pitch: Do it well, and you'll get the next job; fail to satisfy, and you won't. We are always selling when we're trying to get money.

And sometimes on the job, we also ask for money. We ask for money directly when we request a raise or, if self-employed, when we send out a bill; we ask for it indirectly when we want a change of assignment, or a relocation, or a transfer. These strategies for madness-free selling and madness-free asking are aimed at helping you get more money—with less stress and discomfort.

It Starts with Awareness

- If you haven't made vice president by 40, forget it.
- Don't do anything that might get you fired.
- The boss is the enemy.
- It's only a job, you can always get another, don't sweat the small stuff.
- The company owns you.
- Without an advanced degree, you'll never make more than _____.

Do any of these sound familiar? Work messages are inherent in our culture, and we absorb them as early as childhood: a restaurant chain called T.G.I. Friday's (for thank God it's Friday), images of professionals heading for the bar after work to take the edge off, songs about how awful Monday is. If your working parent came home night after night looking drained, with slumping shoulders and circles under the eyes, chances are you grew up with the message that work is tedious drudgery to be endured—five days of misery to get to the weekend. If your working parent spent long hours on the job and seemed focused on work even at home, maybe you grew up with the ingrained idea that work is where the excitement and fulfillment of life are to be found.

Reach back into your childhood and find the work messages you received. Think about how these messages about getting money color and inform your current behavior on the job—my tailspin, Lucy's self-sabotage, Bruce's deliberate ignorance.

Armed with your new awareness, turn your focus to the work part of your money madness. When you walk into the workplace tomorrow, cross the threshold knowing what kind of work message you carry: Somebody else is always making more money. It's just a job. I'd rather be someplace else. The pay sucks and my boss is a jerk.

Then, try behaving just the opposite, as you did back in Chapter 4 when you were taming your money monster. If you're always looking over your shoulder for people who make more money than you do, walk into work tomorrow with the sense that you are overpaid. If you think your boss is a jerk, give yourself the assignment of identifying three qualities in him or her that you admire. If you believe this is "just a job," write an ad for your position that presents your job as the most desirable in the world—and don't lie. Read the ad first thing every morning when you get to work.

Ask yourself how you would behave at work if you did not have the childhood work message and the particular money madness you have—and act accordingly. Changing behavior can bring you eye to eye with your money monster so you can allow yourself to feel your difficult feelings, relax into them, and free yourself of your money madness.

Work the Numbers

I might have saved myself from the distress of that tailspin back in the old days if only I had looked at some numbers. The fact is that losing your money madness about work requires answers to a few simple questions: What are you giving to the job? What are you getting from it? Is the one worth the other? But in calculating an answer to these questions, salary or wage level is not the sole consideration—that is, it's not the sole *financial* consideration.

For example, I could have tried to determine whether my higher-paid colleague had as good a health insurance plan as I had—a benefit that carries a significant financial value. I could have explored the colleague's commute—and what it cost on a daily basis in money, time, and energy. I could have checked out the colleague's retirement plan: Did it offer as many asset classes as my plan? Did it perform as well? Did the company match my colleague's contributions?

I should also have looked at my own future potential earnings. What kind of raise was I due for at my next review—and what was the pattern of annual increases I could look forward to? Maybe, if I calculated the amount I was set to make over the next 5, 10, or 15 years, my colleague's current salary differential wouldn't have looked quite as stunning. Maybe. But because I never looked at the facts, I just continued to get tossed around in that high-emotion tailspin.

Keep in mind that compensation is a package of items that constitute payment for value given. You can assess your value in several ways: Check with the Bureau of Labor Statistics or troll such online job sites as www.Monster.com to see the pay range for your particular job; talk to people who hold equivalent jobs in other companies or other industries; read the classifieds in the local paper. Adjust those figures to include the amount of experience you bring to the work, or your special training, or what you consider a particular skill or added value. But it's also useful, in reckoning both sides of the payment-for-value equation, to look beyond the wage or salary figure given. Ask a friend, spouse, or partner to help by offering his or her perspective. Another view will often look past your own personal blind spots and can remove bias from your calculations.

Bottom line? Get the numbers. Yes, it may take some time to gather the needed facts. On the other hand, I've seen friends spend more time and effort researching and comparing features, capabilities, and prices of high-def TVs than of which job to take. Yet chances are there's no TV without the job compensation to pay for it. Besides, it's a question of perspective: a $1,500 television versus millions of dollars in lifetime earnings.

Selling isn't just for sales professionals. Whatever your job, you are in the selling game. School janitor or university professor, paralegal or computer technician, surgeon or costume designer, every day on the job, you are putting your abilities, your talents, your eagerness, and your performance up for judgment, review, and criticism—and expecting payment in return. And traditionally, when you're trying to make a sale, emotions rule. So as you study my approach for selling the madness-free way, keep in mind that it isn't just about selling a product or service in the marketplace; adapt it to your situation, changing the terms *buyer* and *seller* to *me* and *the boss* or to whatever fits.

I formed the core of this madness-free sales strategy by figuratively sitting at the feet of a master salesman. In fact, he was a client who was shocked at the way I tried to sell him my services and offered to help me structure my approach. The key to it, he told me, was to take emotion out of the process. What he taught me was how.

It was clear I needed some help. By the time I met this client, I was pretty tired of taking things personally every time I went into a sales meeting with a prospect. Just about anything a prospect said would trigger some unproductive emotional response from me. I'd be going along nicely, delivering my presentation, and suddenly the prospective client would interrupt me: "What do you think about that biotech stock everyone's talking about?" he might ask. And I would suddenly feel a tug of fear that I was losing the contest. So I would talk even louder and promise even more. If I sensed that a prospect was losing interest, I would speed up the presentation, offer services I would be challenged to provide, and of course, lower my fee. It was exhausting, and it was singularly ineffective.

I felt, rightly, that I had absolutely no control over these sales meetings, which seemed to be all over the place. Despite all my expertise, all my brochures, all my binders full of colorful flip charts showing portfolio performance, it was the prospect who set the tone of the meeting and governed the agenda. I felt like a servant, there to do the bidding of the prospective client and responding like an emotional pinball to every emotional trigger. *Tilt!*

Eventually, I learned how to be completely relaxed and in the seat of power at every meeting. Paradoxically, the buyer at the meeting is also in the seat of power. The trick is to look at the whole selling process—whatever you're selling—as a *collaboration*, not a contest. Make it a partnership of equals instead of a battle to beat an adversary, and you find yourself in a mutually involving process that seeks the best possible result for both seller and buyer.

How do you do that? By trying for no.

Try for No

Statistics prove the point. In the business of sales, chances are, for example, that for every 10 prospects you call on, 9 will most likely say no, and 1 will say yes. That makes it a numbers game. The unsuccessful salesperson goes after the yes every time, casting the net wide and expending resources and energy and hours across that wide net for just a 1-in-10 shot.

The successful seller will be looking for no, because every no he gets takes him closer to that one yes—and thus gets him there faster. It's like doctors who run a slew of diagnostic tests to eliminate possibilities; each negative result is actually a step toward an accurate diagnosis and therefore to a cure. Ironically, getting a no increases the likelihood of eventually getting a yes.

Why does trying for no work? Because it breaks the traditional pattern, creating a counterpoint to the sense of desperation that seems inherent in selling and waking up the buyer to pay attention in a fresh way. In neutralizing that desperation, you as the seller become a collaborative consultant rather than a supplicant forced into an adversarial position. Over time, as you practice creating this counterpoint, you really do become indifferent to the duality of the yes-or-no confrontation. And the consequence of that indifference is that you relax the buyer, your proposition becomes more appealing, and ironically, you therefore often make more money.

So the very first thing to do if you are to sell successfully is to get comfortable with hearing no. Think about performers who endlessly attend auditions and are endlessly rejected. I have actor and singer friends who say they're inured to being told no at auditions, others who say they never get used to it, and still others who will be on their shrinks' couches for years figuring it out—but they all go back, time after time, audition after audition. They know they have to be comfortable with no, and perhaps they also know instinctively that every no gets them closer to that yes for a role that will put them over the top at last.

I don't expect you to attain the struggling actor's familiarity with no, but I do mean that you must literally get comfortable hearing it. The reason is simple: You're going to hear it a lot. No is normal, just as a down investment market is normal, just as not meeting every goal in your annual strategic plan is normal—and only by expecting no will you succeed. The rejection is not of you; it is of the service or product or argument or proposition that you are offering.

Start now by asking your spouse and/or friends to role-play with you. Make a request of them, have them look you in the eye, and feel the brunt of the rejection targeted directly at you till you're okay with hearing no.

Then go out and look for no. An early no is better than a late no, so you can save your time and energy for the next attempt that may lead to yes.

The Madness-Free Sell-Anything Strategy

Here's how—a five-step strategy for selling anything.

Step I
Connect and Collaborate

Most people walk into a selling situation and give away everything they have to offer. "Here's what I'm going to do for you!" they trumpet, thus yielding up all their power at the outset. How can you tell a buyer what you're offering till you know what the buyer wants? Instead, your goal should be to try for a collaboration, not a win, a sense of partnership, not a conquest. The best way to do that is to start off by establishing an agreement between you on two points: first, that you're both here to see if there is a fit between you, a meeting of the minds; second, that if there is a fit, there will be a defined next step.

Make sure the understanding is clear: There are only two outcomes possible at the end of this meeting. Outcome one is that there is no fit, and you as the seller will recommend another seller who may be more helpful to the prospective client. Outcome two is that the two of you go forward to the agreed-upon next step—maybe another meeting, or a phone call, or a sale. If you cannot get the buyer to commit to a defined next step, it's time to escape the meeting, take the no, and look for another buyer and another meeting.

Achieving this clarity is critical. It keeps you focused on the real issue, which is seeing whether or not there is a fit between you.

Step 2
Cards on the Table

Acknowledge one worry or concern that you imagine might obstruct or undermine the collaboration you seek. That immediately takes away the emotion and counters any desperation you might feel to sell at all costs. A Sikh colleague of mine would start a conversation with a prospect by expressing concern "that my turban might get in the way of our doing business." It was instantly disarming, and it took the fact of his ethnic and cultural difference out of the equation.

Maybe the prospective customer for your handcrafted furniture is dressed to the nines. Tell him you hope your casual attire won't signal a lack of seriousness; rather, these are your work clothes, and you create a better product when you're dressed this way. Maybe the client for your dog-walking service is a woman and you fear she'd be more comfortable with a female dog handler. Say so. I run a company that is very highly regarded but is hardly a household name; I like to bring that up in a sales meeting before the client can. It takes the sting out of the fact; it lets prospects see that I have nothing to hide, there's nothing to fear, and I'm offering authenticity in trying to create a collaboration with him or her. It also puts the focus squarely on me and my company, which is an obvious plus for the selling process.

Get the buyer's cards on the table as well. What has brought him or her to this meeting? What's the motivation? The incentive? The emotional need? The answers tell you what is real for the buyer and will help shape your sales proposition when you finally make it.

Suppose you're interviewing for a job as executive assistant. Ask why there's an opening. The previous executive assistant left? After only six months? Why? What happened—and how did your inter-viewer feel about it?

Remember: You're a collaborator, trying to find out what's going on. So put it all out there. Get naked. Deflate the fears before they surface. Having all cards on the table lets you get to a good collaboration—or if necessary, to a no—efficiently and effectively.

Step 3
The Fee or Price

What do you want to get from the collaboration? It is essential for you as the seller to bring up the issue rather than waiting for the buyer to do so. The reason? Money is *so* emotional—which is why you're reading this book. Bringing it up on your own takes the charge out of it; when that happens, the buyer listens more closely and can hear you more clearly.

Say it outright: "My fee is in the x-thousand dollar range; is that a barrier to us working together?" Or, in the case of a nonmonetary transaction: "I have a 30-minute presentation; I'd like the audience's full attention. Will that be a problem for you?" For the most part, buyers will say it is not a problem or there is no barrier because they're intrigued to hear what you have to offer. But if price is an is-sue, you're better off resolving it or taking the no and moving on.

For you as the seller, stating the price now means you don't have to be tempted to discount it at the end of the transaction, when your selling power is at its lowest ebb.

Step 4
Solutions and Resolution

Tell the buyer how you will solve each of his problems. Then ask the buyer if your solutions work for him.

In the interview for the executive assistant's job, pull out your c.v. to demonstrate your record of longevity in previous jobs. Ask the in-terviewer if such persistence doesn't answer his concern. Then stay silent as you wait for his yes.

Offer your prospective dog-walking client a list of other women customers who will testify to your gentle ways with canines. You're collaborating with this client: You feel her need and can address it. Ask, "Does that address your concern about me as your dog-walker?" Smile, say nothing, and wait for yes.

Step 5
Next?

The last and simplest step in the madness-free sell-anything strategy is simply to ask the buyer: "What do we do next?" Put the power in your prospective buyer's hands. Go silent.

What you expect is a definite commitment—either a sale or a secure appointment to continue the process. Wait for it. Don't prompt the buyer. Don't help him. Don't make a suggestion. If you get the commitment, well and good, you've gotten your yes.

If the buyer says he'd like to "get back to you next week," gently remind him of your commitment in Step 1 to a "go" or "no go" course of action. If he still hems and haws, suggest that this is not a fit. Offer to refer him to someone else, and ask if he can refer you to other prospects. In other words, deliver your own no, bringing you closer to yes.·

Billing Clients: The Nightmare of the Self-Employed

However you set out to get money, at some point, you pretty much have to ask for it. In selling, you need to state your price. In asking for a job, you need to demand a living wage. And if you run your own business, you eventually need to bill your clients. For an awful lot of us, money madness makes any kind of asking for money difficult, but of course, it's the bottom-line essential of making a living.

Elizabeth is 40, a talented, skilled graphic artist who works freelance—as a self-employed, independent contractor—as more and more Americans seem to be doing these days. She is highly educated in the liberal arts and highly trained in her profession, so when she told her story in a recent workshop, it was confirmation yet again that intelligence and erudition afford no special advantage in the fight against money madness.

The story this supremely capable woman told, tearfully, was that she spends more time figuring out what to charge for a job than actually doing the work. She panics about how to count the hours she has put in. *I took a break to answer the phone,* she thinks. *How shall I subtract that from the total?*

She worries constantly about what rate to charge, about whether her fees are competitive within her industry, about whether the job she did really represents the best she could do, about whether she should treat the small client like a nonprofit and charge less, or whether it's fair to make up the difference by charging a big company more.

Caught between the twin fears of being rejected by the client on the one hand and simply going broke on the other, Elizabeth approaches each invoice as if it were an infectious and possibly fatal disease.

It's the nightmare of the self-employed, and it's all too familiar to me. I've written about how difficult I found it, when I first started out as a wealth advisor, to set a fee for my services. It's tough to hit the right note, especially when you're inexperienced. Too high, I worried, and I'd lose the gig. Too low, and my business would no longer be sustainable. But mostly, of course, I was being driven by my money monster's need for security and his prohibition on talking openly about money—two necessities that did not easily square with one another in a sales meeting.

Elizabeth had her own money madness, of course. We learned in the workshop that she could get away with undervaluing her work because her father continued to help support her. He loved his daughter very much, and he expressed his love in money—enough money to subsidize her asking for the lowest fees possible.

What Elizabeth was able to discover in the workshop was that charging the right amount for her work—valuing the work itself—would separate her from her father. Simply put, she feared that if she became financially independent, she would lose her special relationship with him.

Of course, Elizabeth's money monster had a field day with this. If money is love, then I must keep my father's money; to compensate for keeping my father's money, I must undervalue—even disparage—my work and my profession. No wonder Elizabeth approached the whole subject of billing with dread and a feeling of doom; every invoice stirred stress at the very depths of her being.

Madness-Free Billing: Get the Emotion Out of the Invoice

Clearly, Elizabeth's fretting over what to charge had nothing whatsoever to do with her client or her work. By the same token, my inability to state my price loud and clear was not a result of weak vocal cords. In both cases, the issue was our money madness. That is why the only real cure for the invoicing quandary among the self-employed is to do the work of awareness that is the foundation of curing money madness. And it is why the first step toward madness-free invoicing is simply to remind yourself that you are not really agonizing over a bill but over your blind clinging to a childhood money message.

Still, there are practical interim steps you can take at once to get you out of the emotionally fraught process. Apply these steps as you do the work of curing your money madness until you're able to charge for your work as objectively as if you were a third party.

One interim step, in fact, is to turn the whole task over to a third party. Hire a billing firm or a personal representative or a high school kid who is good with numbers to compute, mail out, and follow up on your bills.

But even a third party cannot do an effective job unless and until you establish a set of rules and standards. Rules and standards are what free you from fretting and enable you to focus your energy more productively on the work. That's why big companies have huge standards manuals; they ensure consistency, fairness, and accuracy time after time.

You'll need written rules about whether or not to charge for the time taken for that phone call. About how you'll itemize out-of-pocket expenses. Will you offer a *pro bono* discount for nonprofits? Will you charge a premium for work the client asks you to do over the weekend or on a tightly compressed schedule?

To figure out how to set these rules and standards, start by asking colleagues what they do. If you don't know any colleagues personally, check out the yellow pages or attend the next conference or convention of people in your line of work and ask.

And while standards and rules must play a role in determining what to charge, in the end, the price you ask must reflect the value you provide. That in itself comprises a number of factors.

- *What you need to live on.* You're in this business to make a living. So pay yourself fairly. One good way to ensure this is to open a separate business bank account that keeps business expenses distinct from your personal expenses; then pay yourself a salary that the business can afford—no matter how minimal. Over time, as you track income and outgo, you'll get greater clarity on whether to bill more or less in order to stay in business—or find another way to make a living.

- *The value you're producing for the client.* If you're a graphic artist producing a logo that will brand the company in all its communications worldwide, that is likely to be a more valuable contribution than a one-off image you produce for a brochure. Your work will be used more widely and will last longer in branding the company than the one-off; it therefore requires more of the graphic artist and delivers more to the client—and more should be paid.

- *The unique value you bring to the job.* All of us have a genius quality—something we love doing that we do better than most. You're bringing yours to this work, and that's worth paying for. You are not a commodity your client has plucked off the shelf; you are a unique individual who brings to the task a very specific creative intelligence, skill and training, and a particular body of experience.

- *Industry standards.* When you undercharge, you hurt the client as well. As I have experienced—and others have confirmed—billing too low can diminish the value of the work performed. I might rush a bit more than I should, or feel less accountable for high quality, or feel more indifferent to the client. So check out industry standards, and use them as a guide.

As for Elizabeth, I'm happy to report that the two-day workshop brought her sufficient clarity that she has begun to work through her relationship with her father. The clarity has also empowered her to remove her own emotions from the billing process, which, for the moment, she has agreed to contract out to an objective, professional, third-party billing agency.

Asking for Money: The Madness-Free Raise Request

Asking for a raise is a little bit like selling and a little bit like asking for money. You have the best chance of achieving the resolution you want if you can make the request into a collaboration between you and the raise-granting boss. Bring awareness of your money madness with you so that you don't take the verdict personally—whether a yes or a no.

One thing to keep in mind when you approach your supervisor about a raise is that the supervisor is inclined to do what makes sense for *her*. Your aim in creating a collaboration between the two of you, therefore, is to persuade the boss that what makes sense for her is a good raise for you. The right raise will keep you on the job, highly motivated, and high performing—and that's good for the boss's performance, job security, and career growth as well.

Prepare for any madness-free raise request by being certain you walk into the meeting or performance review with solid data in hand. First, you want data on comparable compensation—that is, the kinds of raises people in equivalent jobs in the same region of the country are getting this year. If the going increase is 4 percent, you might be way off base asking for 15 percent.

The second set of data you want is a clear articulation of the value you have created for the company over the past year—in measurable, dollars-and-cents terms. You want to be able to define for the boss exactly how you have contributed to the department's success—and therefore to the boss's success—or how you helped mitigate any failures.

Begin creating your collaboration when you schedule the meeting. If the boss wants a review for Wednesday morning, but that's when you're supposed to be working with the team on the presentation for the sales conference, say so. It not only establishes you as an equal partner with important commitments, it also shows your conscientiousness.

In the meeting, start the selling strategy. Connect and get an understanding from the boss about the outcome you both agree the meeting should produce. Probe the boss's motivations and incentives for giving you a raise, and be truthful and clear—get naked—about your own motivations and incentives. If the boss tells you why you should get a raise, it's more effective than if you tell the boss.

But don't state your price; let the boss do that first. Set it up by telling the boss that you value your work here, you value the company, you believe your work adds value to the company's goals, and you'd like to know what kind of raise the boss has in mind for you "to see if it makes sense for both of us."

If it turns out that the boss's idea of what makes sense is less than yours, this is the moment to use the data you've brought with you. If the boss has offered a 5 percent raise and the industry is giving 7 percent this year for the kind of job you have, tell the boss exactly that—and maybe negotiate for a nonmonetary equivalent: a corner office or more vacation time. Present your dollars-and-cents measurement of the value you brought to the company this year, and suggest that such value deserves a higher reward than the boss has stated. As best you can, stay neutral and nondesperate—remember, this isn't a contest—and let the boss do the talking.

And if your request is still not granted, set an agenda for another review and ask for a clear list of what you must achieve to earn a particular increase in a stated amount of time. With such an agreement, you're both committed as professional partners, and there's no room for the emotions of money madness.

Work isn't the only way to get money. Some people also inherit it, and some people who are going to inherit money often ask for it in advance as a loan or a gift. What I call the "inheritance conversation" is one I think all parents and their grown children should have—and one I absolutely advise all my clients to undertake sooner rather than later. That's the conversation in which children discuss what, if anything, they and their siblings, if any, can expect in terms of an inheritance, and in which parents can make recommendations, if they so choose, about ways their children might spend, save, or give away the inheritance.

I've seen time and again among my clients what happens when that conversation is *not* held, and I offer it as an article of faith that it's a lot better to have no surprises on this issue when you and your siblings are in the midst of grief and mourning. When the inheritance is less than expected, confusion is added to grief, and grown men and women may feel a sense of betrayal and wonder whether Mommy and Daddy really loved them. Oddly, when the inheritance is greater than expected, a sense of resentment can creep in: "I could have used this money earlier." "Is this to compensate for the love that was withheld?"

I've also seen cases in which the distribution of the inheritance was unequal, the parents assuming that their neurosurgeon child wouldn't need or care about the money whereas the poet child would clearly need help. Invariably, the neurosurgeon will feel that the poet was more loved, and invariably, sibling relations will be strained—often past the point of recall.

I've also seen countless times what happens when the conversation *is* held, and I have been impressed at how adult children exhibit real satisfaction with lowered expectations, so long as they have been informed of those expectations in advance.

So hold the inheritance conversation now—while all parties can speak and be heard.

Or maybe you're an adult child who wants to ask your well-heeled parents for money "ahead of time." As awkward moments go, such a request can be right up there with billing your clients or asking for a raise. In fact, asking for what is effectively an advance on your inheritance can be particularly fraught, for there's no way to avoid the subject of your parents' deaths—and such a reminder is probably not the best way to tap someone for a handout. What's more, the subject can bring up all kinds of family and personal issues, many of which may never have been raised before. That's why the first thing you say should be an acknowledgment of that very fact.

"I know this is a difficult subject," you might begin, "and I suspect you might think that I don't work hard enough (didn't go into the right profession, don't know the value of a dollar). But I'd like to know how you might feel about giving me some of my inheritance now."

Then listen. Having disarmed your parents with your candor and having asked for their views, you must hear them out.

When you finally do present your request, frame it in terms of a disciplined proposal, and make clear to them that what you are asking for is not the fish, as the proverb goes, but the means to learn how to fish. That is, you are asking for resources that will enable you to achieve something independently; you are not seeking to depend on them for wherewithal into an indefinite future.

Maybe you want to start a business; come equipped with a business plan. Maybe you'd like to live closer to them in their old age and can't afford the housing in the area. Perhaps you want to take a year off to pursue a humanitarian goal. Show them the facts about the goal, where you would pursue it, the organization through which you would work.

Finally, to guide your responses to them during this conversation, put yourself in your parents' shoes. Imagine your own children all grown up and coming to ask you for money. Ask yourself how you would respond—and act accordingly.

In this as in all aspects of getting money, clarity in looking at the facts and communicating openly about the facts are essential. Take a Money Breath—before the job interview, the sales call, the inheritance conversation—break the pattern, go counter to conditioning and culture, and you'll find you'll get more money.

CHAPTER 8

Madness-Free Spending

Spending may be the most automatic of our money activities. Our consumer society constantly assures us that buying things is good for us. And then it makes it abundantly easy to do—with credit cards, debit cards, PayPal, swiping, and the like. Shopping has become a pastime, a form of entertainment—right up there with a golf game or a movie or dinner with good friends as a desirable way to spend time. We do it casually, impulsively buying whatever catches our fancy—whether a new blouse, or a new car, or sometimes even a new house. But as we all know, such emotion-driven shopping carries the curse of money madness. It can cause us distress, may keep us from getting the things we truly value, and robs us of joy.

So in this chapter, I'll present some ideas for spending in a madness-free way, whether you're shopping at the mall—especially if you're relying on your credit card as you shop—or approaching a very big-ticket expenditure like a home.

The Seductions of Shopping

The Athenians had the Agora, the Romans had the Forum, we Americans have the mall—both the physical and the online. We love to shop. We believe—because our consumer society drums it into our heads—that buying things will transform our lives. Owning this item or that will bring us fulfillment. Possessing all these attractive, available things will make us happy. We will become smarter, stronger, braver, better—if only we acquire the things that are there to acquire.

I remember a wonderful billboard ad for BMW cars I saw a couple of years ago. Over an image of a sleek sports coupe that seemed to be *vrooming* through the kind of landscape where rich people live on large estates was this tagline: "Adrenaline comes standard." Brilliant in its simplicity, the tagline had the added virtue of unvarnished honesty. BMW was admitting that it wasn't really selling a ton of steel engineered to convey you from one place to another; rather, it was selling you a *feeling*—excitement perhaps at powering that particular ton of steel, or satisfaction at acquiring the prestigious BMW brand, or hope that owning the car ranked you among the estate owners in that lovely countryside on the billboard. What the ad made clear was that it was aiming for your emotions. Period.

It's money madness, of course. And our money monster can be relied on to egg us on to that excitement we feel when we want an object and know we are going to get it. A Buddhist monk I know speaks of the sheer exaltation we feel at the moment *just before* we actually pay for it. Try to notice this in yourself the next time you're at the counter about to hand over cash or the credit card; track when the money madness kicks in—the exhilarating moment of heightened expectation that is nothing less than thrilling, not unlike the surge of emotion investors feel when they get a hot tip on a can't-lose investment. **In fact, there's a case to be made that we crave the feeling more than the object itself. That is money madness in a nutshell.**

The problem comes when the purchase has been made. Letdown sets in, as it is likely to do because the purchase was directed by the emotions of our particular money madness. The result is distress, its form dependent on the nature of your particular money madness. Maybe you feel buyer's remorse, maybe you're angry that your life has not been transformed by the purchase, maybe it just makes you want to own more.

So how can we spend without such distress? How can we achieve madness-free shopping?

See Through the Seductions

The first approach is to find a way to pass through the onslaught of advertising and marketing and peer pressure unscathed—without feeling the compulsion to spend money for the sake of the things it can buy. It's tough; it's a little like asking: "How do you resist the irresistible?"

Start by taking a Money Breath. This will reawaken your awareness, and the trick for shopping is to focus your new awareness of money madness on our consumerist culture. Knowing what you now know about your own personal money madness, you can begin to understand why you react as you do to all the gadgets and gizmos; clothes and shoes; accessories, chess sets, travel clocks, gardening and do-it-yourself tools, and sports gear—all the goods and chattel, paraphernalia, and accouterments available to us in malls and in mail-order catalogs and on website after website.

You can concentrate your awareness on analyzing the supposed advantage you will gain by buying these things—and then buying them and buying them and buying them some more. What is the deficiency that your money monster assures you will be filled by this flat-screen computer monitor or that handbag or the fully featured, customizable, portable GPS? What is the particular craving—for recognition, wealth, security, glamour, the chance to stand out from the pack—that your money monster says will be satisfied if only you buy the item?

When I first moved to California to open the West Coast branch of Abacus Wealth Partners, I decided—or rather, my money monster decided—that I needed a laptop for all the traveling back and forth between my East Coast and West Coast offices. The idea was to be productive while hanging out in airport lounges and while staying in numerous hotel rooms. Important businesspeople who travel all have laptops. It's how they stay connected. In fact, it's today's essential CEO accessory, and my money monster was not about to let me leave home without it. In fact, nothing less than a top-of-the-line laptop would do, with a full complement of bells and whistles—plus the handsome backpack with the specially padded laptop compartment and neat slots for all the peripherals I was buying.

The logic of this money madness was that unless I had *all* the tools—hardware, software, accessories, gadgets, and doohickeys—I might miss out on some essential capability, might cheat myself out of some latent and as yet undiscovered potential. *This is your security blanket!* my money monster told me. *Without it, you might not be seen as a real player!*

I am looking at the backpack now, the laptop and all its accessories within it, as I sit here writing with a ballpoint pen on a legal pad. For within a month or so, and after two airplane trips with the laptop, I found that it was annoyingly inconvenient to take the thing through airport security, that the screen was too small, that I worried about battery life, and that the technology itself, while impressive, was overkill for my needs. Moreover, the laptop sort of constituted a self-fulfilling prophecy—that is, because it was there, I felt compelled to turn it on once the plane was airborne, rather than using the travel time to do something else—or nothing at all.

Once again, I had allowed my fears about security—my usually dormant money madness—to drive me to do the thing that was totally wrong for me. My craving to stand out from the pack went unfulfilled; in fact, since all I had done was waste money, the whole transaction was counterproductive, making me feel less successful than ever.

I offer it as an object lesson. Ask yourself what you're really buying; if some of what you're trying to obtain is power, prestige, love, or identity, it's your money madness doing the buying, not you.

A Range, Not a Budget

A second strategy can complement and supplement this awareness and put an end to the budgeting fiasco. You know what the budgeting fiasco is, don't you? Most personal finance books and advisors tell us to make a budget and stick to it. That's like saying go on a diet and stick to it, or draw up a schedule and stick to it. Sounds good, but then we're invited to dinner at the home of friends, and the hostess insists her feelings will be hurt if we don't eat her homemade chocolate cake. There goes the diet. Or we become hopelessly mired in a traffic jam, and there goes the schedule.

The budgeting fiasco works the same way. We've duly established a monthly budget number for discretionary expenses, but there we are at the mall, and there's that full-featured, customizable, portable GPS staring us in the face. Our money monster is instantly stirred into action, and suddenly, the monthly budget for discretionary expenses has been blitzed.

The bottom line is that budgeting doesn't work and causes stress.

We're constantly renegotiating with ourselves; rationalizing and justifying spending that busts the budget; feeling guilty; getting angry and resentful over what we see as budget limits; experiencing buyer's remorse, shame, self-pity, and anxiety. **This isn't a solution to our money madness; it's an offshoot of it.**

The first line of attack against the budgeting fiasco is the monthly cash flow. Remember back in Chapter 5 when you tracked those expenses? Here it is again, only this time with room for you to state your spending *intentions*—the least amount you think is reasonable for what's needed and the most you can afford to spend on the category. For some of the categories—mortgage payment or rent, for example—a range will not be feasible; these are fixed for now, so your low and high monthly intentions would be the same. But for everything else, set yourself a range.

Your Monthly Spending Intentions		
Fixed Spending	**Low Monthly Intention**	**High Monthly Intention**
Housing		
Mortgage/rent		
Property taxes and homeowner's/renter's insurance		
Savings for long-term repairs/improvements		
Maintenance and cleaning		
Utilities		
Other		
Housing total		

Fixed Spending	Low Monthly Intention	High Monthly Intention
Household		
Savings for goals		
Groceries		
Medical/dental		
Education		
Credit card/other loan payments		
Attorney, CPA, and other professional fees		
Household necessities (pet care, toiletries, dry cleaning, personal care, and so on)		
Computer/cell phone		
Health, life, disability, and long-term care insurance		
Other		
Household total		
Transportation		
Car payment		
Car insurance		
Gas		
Parking		

Fixed Spending	Low Monthly Intention	High Monthly Intention
Maintenance, repairs		
Public transportation		
Other		
Transportation total		
Total fixed expenses		
Flexible Spending		
Clothing		
Home furnishings		
Entertainment/vacations		
Charity		
Gifts		
Fitness		
Personal growth		
Other		
Total flexible expenses		
TOTAL EXPENSES (total fixed expenses + total flexible expenses)		
TOTAL INCOME (net take-home pay + investment income)		
NET CASH FLOW (total income—total expenses)		

Thinking in terms of intention and range completely changes the psychology engendered in you by the relentless fixed point of a budget. A budget number is a limit—"I will spend only $200 on clothing this month, no matter what!" Or "I will spend not a penny more than $75 on running shoes at the mall today. Period!" By contrast, a range offers a field of choice—say, a monthly clothing spending intention of $175 to $225, or running shoe options from $55 to $75. And where a budget is hard to stick to and rather easy to break or go around, a range has a wide girth that's tougher to avoid and that offers some give under pressure.

A low-to-high range gives you more information as you approach any kind of spending and lets you plan your spending in a whole new way. With a fixed budget, we tend to want to fill the cup right to the brim; if we budget $4,000 for a vacation, we look for a resort that will cost exactly that—and it usually ends up costing more. If instead we're looking at a range from $3,000 to $4,000, our minds tend to be satisfied with the middle of the range, so we end up spending less. And it is certainly less stressful to deal with a range of possibilities than to be focused on a single number. It's also more fun, which may be why it's more successful.

So now that you know your intentions for your overall monthly spending, apply the same concept to your shopping for specific items. And next time you head out to the mall, toss out the budget and instead think in terms of range. Suppose you're shopping for a new business suit for work, winter jackets for the kids, and a bike helmet. What's the range for total spending—the least amount of money you could reasonably spend today and the most you can afford—and within that, what is the range for each item on the list? Obviously, when you add up the top numbers for all the separate items, that total must not exceed the top of your range for the full day's spending. But below that ceiling, you have a field of choices.

My recommendation is to write your range on a piece of paper. Carry it with you to the mall. When the GPS heats up your blood, take a Money Breath, as always, remind yourself about the last item that heated your blood and ask yourself if it made you as happy as you had hoped, and check the piece of paper with your spending range on it. Keep checking it. A realistic dollar range will lower the stress associated with shopping—and keep you madness-free.

The Debt Dilemma

It's no secret that one of the great enablers of the kind of spending driven by money madness is easy credit—represented most dramatically by the profligate use of credit cards—which has brought us as a nation to a historic level of consumer debt. Each year, Americans charge $2 trillion on their credit cards, using them to pay for everything from appliances to restaurant meals to the repaving of the driveway and nursery school tuition.

The credit card has become the essential all-American accessory, and getting your first credit card has become a rite of passage akin to getting your driver's license. College freshmen get an instant education in how to plunge into debt as they are bombarded by seductive offers, personally addressed to them, of no-interest-for-three-months credit cards. By the time they're sophomores, many are already behind the debtor's eight ball, and far too many of our finest graduates start their work lives deeply in debt not just to the banks that have granted them student loans but to the consumer credit card companies as well. It's a burden that may take them years to unload.

No wonder debt has become a pressing concern at all ages. It is an oppressive burden that at the very least adds stress to people's lives—and at worst can send them into bankruptcy court or financial disaster.

Let me be clear: There is nothing inherently wrong with debt. It is not immoral; moreover, at times, it may be useful and advisable to go into debt. Debt can be a safety valve in a time of emergency or difficulty; in a crisis, especially one that may be life-threatening, it is a blessing to be able to confront a necessary expense knowing that you can pay it over time. Similarly, if a life-enhancing opportunity presents itself, it is a boon to know you have the ability to seize it by paying for it in installments.

Debt, in short, makes it possible for us to reach beyond our immediate circumstances to gain something important—it's how the vast majority of us can own our own home, buying an asset that can pay us back in time—at the price of being bound to pay for it into the future. That future obligation, of course, constitutes the risk inherent in debt, and the risk is present whether the debt is secured to an underlying asset, like your house in the case of a mortgage, or is entirely unsecured. But overall, in both theory and fact, the ability to assume debt can be a useful thing.

But the current ease with which far too many of us go into debt today—especially consumer credit debt—constitutes an abuse of that good. As the subprime mortgage crisis has shown, and as tens of thousands of individual cases of foreclosure and bankruptcy confirm, such abuse has a very deleterious impact indeed.

And here's the truth of the matter: No book, no money guru, no amount of financial advice can keep you from getting into that kind of debt or get you out of that kind of debt. The reason is simple: Such debt isn't a money issue; it's a money madness issue.

Remember my friend Steve from the very beginning of this book? He was in credit card debt up to his neck back when he made $30,000 a year. He now pulls in about $2 million a year—and his level of credit card debt has risen to well above his ears. Clearly, money is not the problem. Steve's money madness is the problem—some blind, irrational, reckless impulse driving him to behavior that will always keep him behind the debtor's eight ball, unless and until he cures the madness.

I have another friend, Doug, who last year arranged an ambitious African safari vacation for himself and his family. It was top-of-the-line everything—hotels, safari camps, outfitters—in several different countries and through numerous national game parks. And Doug put it all on his credit card. As the family boarded the plane, the anxiety about debt was already stressing Doug out. He never really saw the lions and gazelles, the cheetahs and crocodiles his family saw; all Doug could think about was the bill waiting for him when he got home. Is that any way to go on vacation?

Debt Deceptions

In fact, there may be more irrationality, more lame excuses, more unjustifiable "justifications," more sheer self-deception about debt than about any other financial subject—and it all stems from money madness.

By its very nature, of course, debt is something in the future, and perhaps that is why we childishly assume it will "go away by itself," as one workshop participant once put it. This is a childish response; it isn't just wishful thinking, it's an unwillingness to confront the numbers, to deal with reality in an adult way.

Or we justify going into debt by explaining that we fell in love—with the house, the car, the African safari vacation. Such an explanation has the advantage of making us feel good—who could possibly oppose being in love?—but in fact, falling in love blocks sound reasoning and cuts us off from the rational wisdom we possess.

I've heard people justify a major spike in their credit card debt by saying they "needed" the item—for "survival." That would be true if the item were food or shelter, but it is not true of the $400 wireless reading device, which, although useful and fun to have, has yet to be shown to be essential for basic survival.

"I deserve it." "My earnings will probably be going up, so it's okay to incur debt now." "If they're willing to lend me money, I must be able to afford it." These are some of the other standard rationalizations we offer to ourselves when we plunk down the credit card or apply for the loan, and not one of them is really about money; they're all about our money madness. After all, you may indeed deserve whatever it is you're buying on credit, but what does that have to do with buying it? Your earnings probably will go up in the future, but all you're doing by building up debt is adding more pressure and stress to your future at the same time. And as for turning over all authority over your money to a lending institution, which is what you do when you let it determine what you can or cannot afford, keep in mind that lenders are in business to lend. They know that a certain percentage of loans will go bad, and they do not care if yours is one of them. For them, it's a matter of percentages, and they are structured to minimize losses in the long run. But you lose when you give up your power over your own finances to a lending bank or anyone else.

So while the rationalizations aren't really about money, the consequences, unfortunately, *are*—in stressful, harmful ways. Routinely adding to your consumer debt, as so many of us are doing these days, is like trying to drive without any gas in the tank. The car just won't go. Period.

Dealing with Your Debt

There's only one way to *get* out of debt, and that's to pay it off—or declare bankruptcy. There's only one way to *stay* out of debt, and that's to cure your money madness. Once you do, you'll be able to respond rationally to shopping-by-credit seductions, not with empty rationalizations.

If there's a single benchmark to check yourself against when you may be tempted to add debt to your life, it's your monthly spending intentions statement. It will show you, in black and white, whether there is room in the numbers for you to take on the new expense that the debt repayment requires. When the car salesman tries to persuade you that you're not paying $20,000 for the car, you're paying "only" $350 a month, look to your cash flow statement. Is there an extra $350 a month in those numbers? If not, what are you willing to give up to have the car?

I'll offer one recommendation about credit that can help you get out of debt and stay out of debt. It's this: Give up your credit cards, at least temporarily for purposes of teaching yourself how to live without them. (Well, keep one for emergencies, but stash the others in a locked drawer for the length of time you decide to do without them.) My wife and I tried this a couple of years ago. I had been on a TV news show talking about spending and had publicly cut up my credit cards on the air, declaring that my wife and I would do without them for four months. It was a tremendous experience.

Our values shifted markedly when we could no longer spend in that free-and-easy way that credit cards enable, where you just pull out the card and hand it over. Paying with credit cards, in fact, makes spending an utterly mindless exercise, while counting out the 5s, 10s, and 20s concentrates your mind wonderfully on the matter at hand. One result when you literally lighten your wallet with every purchase is that you are apt to spend less money overall.

The experience was also a wake-up call for us as to what was really important and what came to seem rather trivial, what was worth spending money on and what wasn't. At the same time, the experience enabled us to restore a kind of excitement to our money life that had long been missing—namely, the excitement of saving up for something we wanted. Since we were now spending only what we had in ready cash, it was actually fun to put money aside for a particular purpose: a European cycling vacation, a solid-wood dining table, a fund to provide for our Bijon puppy. We took pleasure in saving for these items, and we seemed to take greater pleasure in possessing the items as well—perhaps precisely because we had, in a way, earned them. To this day, whenever we can, we use cash, checks, or debit cards. I recommend you do the same. Spend like your grandparents spent—when the money is there.

Your Home Is Your Castle

As purchases go, there's nothing bigger than our house. But while home buying is probably the single most significant money decision any of us make in our lifetime, it nevertheless operates on pretty much the same dynamic as any other purchase.

We tend to buy impulsively. We tend not to look at the numbers. We operate from our childhood money messages rather than from current reality, telling ourselves, justifiably, that we have to have a place to live. In other words, money madness governs our purchase of a home, just as it governs our purchase of that GPS or the Kindle or the high-def TV, the cashmere sweater or the laptop.

And home buying is so big it comes with its own cliché: "Your home is your castle." That's at the heart of our money madness about home buying: our house as the asset that will grow in value and as the castle to which and within which we can do pretty much as we please. What's more, having our own home is part of what our culture sees as the standard progression of life: You're born, you go to school, you get a job, you get married, you buy a house, you have kids, you retire.

So it's the standard next step at a certain point in life to start thinking about going to see a real estate agent and checking out what's available. Emotion rides with us as the agent drives us to one property after another, calibrating the ride to show us first the least expensive of the offerings, then crescendoing to the top of the price range as he presents what he tells us is "more your sort of thing." Our childhood money messages are along for the ride as well, feeding our fantasies. Our money monster is there to tell us that this house, not that one, will make us happy, peaceful, successful, the envy of all who drive by. This apartment, not that one, will answer our craving for recognition, our desire for wealth, our need for security. Our money monster has a field day with this moment of decision, sending analysis and deliberation scurrying and letting the formidable power of sheer emotion take over.

I've seen people buy a house in less time, and with less probing of the financial implications, than they apply to buying a car, or membership in a gym, or a microwave oven. But the financial implications are huge: Housing is just about everyone's biggest annual expenditure—for carrying charges or rent, for maintenance, landscaping, repair, renovation, and the like. Whether you live in a 10,000-square-foot mansion or an efficiency condo, your "castle" takes the biggest chunk of your yearly spending—a fact conveniently forgotten when the real estate agent drives up to a place that seems to epitomize your dream of home.

Remember my friend Sandy from Chapter 2? The woman who fell in love with the fireplace in the living room and bought the house on that basis alone? Although a mortgage broker with all the tools of her trade at her command, she performed no financial analysis, barely looked at the other rooms, did no research on utility costs, maintenance, even property taxes. Believe me, if Sandy were shopping for a microwave, she would do due diligence every which way before buying. She would assess cooking power, research the upsides and downsides of convection, compare prices at discount stores and high-end shops. That's much more than she did with her house.

And while there are those cold winter nights when she does indeed sit in front of the fire with her glass of wine, as she dreamed, her pleasure in the house is neutralized somewhat by the financial struggle to keep it, and by the near-certainty that once she is retired and living on a fixed income, Sandy will not be able to keep it after all.

If Sandy had understood the financial struggle her fireplace dream would cost her, she might still have bought her house, but she would have done so with her eyes open to the reality of the sacrifices she would have to make, not to mention the reality of having to sell it someday. That is the price she's paying for being ruled by emotion.

The ideas I present for getting your home don't deny that such emotion exists, but they enable you to resolve the emotion as you examine the true costs of what you'll spend for your home, rationally and sensibly. Whether you're thinking about moving, considering renovating, or hoping to sell a house, the ideas will show you how to determine the true costs. Follow the ideas to madness-free behavior—more witness discipline, less emotion—and you'll make a decision that both is financially sound and gets you a house you'll value on a personal level.

Gimme Shelter

I bought my first house because—well, because it was time. It was the late 1980s, I was a young man on the rise in a solid profession, and that's what one did. It was a Tudor-style townhouse on a leafy block within the city limits of Philadelphia but just steps from the legendary Main Line, with its quaint villages and gracious estates. It was an older house, which I loved. True, I noted that there were instances where "old" was not necessarily an advantage: There were patches of decay in the concrete driveway, for example. But I was crazy about the single-pane casement windows, and I was charmed by the idiosyncrasies of the house, like the fact that when you walked in, the first light switch you encountered was all the way on the other side of the living room.

I did what I thought was all the due diligence needed: found the best deal I could on a mortgage, reckoned my monthly payments and assessed them affordable, and, of course, had the house inspected. The inspection made it clear that the roof would need to be replaced "within 5 to 10 years"; I made a note of the fact but never factored the cost of a new roof into the cost of the house.

Then I moved in. The house was cold. I had bought it in the spring, when most houses are bought and sold, and never thought to explore the issue of insulation; as it turned out, it was old, thin, and worn through in major areas. The lovely old casement windows were letting in a lot of the cold, too; as old as the house, they no longer fit the window openings, which had shifted as the house settled, and the estimated cost to replace them was staggering. The idiosyncratic lighting turned out to be bad wiring bordering on the dangerous, and the whole house needed to be rewired: yet another major-dollar retrofit.

I hadn't thought to save up a contingency cushion while I was putting money aside for a down payment, so all these bills used up all my spare cash and then some, presenting me with the unpleasant choice of giving up some other things I had gotten used to in my life or going into credit card debt, something I have always avoided.

I bought the house for $70,000 in 1987, put about $30,000 into it for repairs and retrofitting, and sold it in 1992 for $96,000. Bottom line? In direct costs, I lost 4,000 bucks on the house; as to the cost of lost opportunity—that is, the gain I might have realized if only I had invested that $30,000 repair bill plus my $20,000 down payment in the Rainbow Portfolio—it's too painful to even calculate, but it was something on the order of a $40,000 gain instead of a $4,000 loss. (The rent I was paying on my previous home was actually less than the monthly mortgage and carrying charges for the house I bought.)

What did I do wrong? Simple. I allowed my emotions to put blinders on me. After all, I'm a financial guy. More than most people, I should have taken care to separate out the emotional considerations—I was at the right point in my career, I liked the windows, loved the Tudor look—from the financial considerations. I should have looked at the financial realities with the cold objectivity for which my profession is supposedly known.

But the truth is that most people don't look at the financial realities when they are considering buying a house—even if they think they do. They think about the tax deduction for mortgage interest, and they calculate what their monthly payment might be if they get a mortgage at this percent or at that percent. And they dream about how they'll build up equity and sell the house later on to fund their retirement.

Quite right, too. Owning a house pays you back. In a robust real estate market, if you sell at the right time, you'll make money on the sale. And actually, if you have taken out a mortgage to buy the home, you'll do even better, for the leverage from having bought with the bank's money can turbo-boost your return. Here's how:

Suppose you buy a $300,000 house. You put down $60,000, pay $9,000 in closing costs, and take out a $240,000 interest-only mortgage. Then suppose the house increases in value to $402,000 over the succeeding six years. So you sell the house for $378,000—the total selling price minus brokerage commissions, and receive a check for $138,000 at the closing—the net proceeds from the sale minus the

$240,000 mortgage. The $138,000 is a doubling of your original down payment investment of $69,000. In other words, the 26 percent increase in the house's value over the six years you lived there becomes a 100 percent return on your investment. That's the power of leverage.

Of course, anything that can turbo-boost the value of your house in one direction can also work in the other direction. My friend Serena, who paid $400,000 for her house, taking out a $320,000 mortgage for the purpose, got caught in the subprime crunch and ended up selling the house for $300,000, losing her $80,000 down payment plus the additional $20,000. In this case, a 25 percent drop in the home value resulted in more than a 100 percent loss of the original investment.

But in general, home ownership builds up equity, qualifies us for a tax deduction on our mortgage payments, and is an investment in our future: The house we buy won't just be our home, it can be the nest egg of a solid return that can fund our retirement.

Getting Real About Real Estate

But that isn't the whole story, and those aren't the only financial considerations to think about.

"I bought a house for the tax deduction."

I can't begin to count the number of times I've heard that. The legendary tax deduction for mortgage interest is a key component of the near-religious awe with which we Americans regard the financial benefit of home ownership.

In fact, the deduction *is* a statement of public policy. It's our government proclaiming that home ownership is a public good, to be encouraged with public funding. What we call a tax deduction is in effect a government-subsidized loan rate. Here's how it works.

Suppose you're in the 25 percent tax bracket and you take out a $100,000 mortgage at 7 percent interest. In the first year of the loan, you'll owe $7,000 in interest. But if you have enough deductions to itemize, you can deduct the interest from your taxes, thus lessening your taxable income by $7,000—let's say from $80,000 a year to $73,000; you're getting a break of 1.75 percent (0.25 tax bracket times 7 percent interest) on the loan interest. That means you're really borrowing at 5.25 percent, not 7 percent. At 5.25 percent, your first year's interest payment is $5,250, so your famous "tax deduction" has saved you $1,750 in interest in the first year of the loan. That's not exactly a staggering amount. In succeeding years, the savings get smaller and smaller as you begin to pay less in interest and more in principal. The tax benefit declines. So as financial benefits go, the tax deduction for mortgage interest is nice, but it's hardly a deal maker. That's why it's important to do the calculations and not let the allure of the tax deduction blind you to the bigger picture.

There's another reality about having a mortgage that some would argue is its real financial benefit—namely, the automatic month-by-month savings structure that a mortgage creates for you. It's like putting part of your allowance into a piggy bank—and knowing you'll pay forfeit if you don't. Over time, as that savings piggy bank—the equity in your home—gets fatter and fatter, you have it to fall back on. It's your emergency stash in a crisis. It's your collateral for a home equity loan, if needed. If and when you sell the house in your later years and move to a less expensive place, it's money in the bank for your retirement. For someone who doesn't have the discipline to save money, taking out a mortgage to buy a house provides the discipline and lets them build up a nest egg for retirement. For some of my clients, Prisoners of Spending who just can't cure their money madness and save anything, my standard and wholehearted recommendation is: Buy a house, and take out a mortgage to do it.

Another consideration is the investment potential of the house you live in. Certainly, a house is quite likely the biggest asset on your family's balance sheet. Yet as investments go, it is by definition concentrated in one asset class—real estate—and in one geographic market, so it cannot offer the diversification you might get from a portfolio of real estate investments, let alone from the Rainbow Portfolio. While such concentration might raise the potential reward, it also raises the potential risk.

What's more, a house is a driver of multiple other costs and benefits to be weighed against one another. The kind of house you buy, the price you pay, the neighborhood it's in all determine a range of other expenses—from the size of the Christmas tip you'll be expected to give the mailman to how you landscape your lawn to the school your children attend and the costs associated with their education. You might own a $250,000 house in a neighborhood where the mail carriers supply preaddressed envelopes for their Christmas tip, and maybe the neighborhood association allows lawn mowing only on weekdays—so you need to hire someone to do it—and maybe the only good school is a high-priced private academy. Or you might own a $400,000 house down a rural lane where nobody cares about your lawn and from which you drive your kids to an excellent public school *en route* to the post office to pick up your mail.

In other words, the house you live in lives in a context, and its total price will be a lot more than the monthly payment.

When I began writing this book, the housing market was still in its boom phase. Since then, the subprime mortgage crisis has cooled the frenzy considerably. Home prices were bid up so high during the boom that future price increases are likely to be smaller. For example, after the housing boom of the 1980s, home prices in many markets fell consistently for the three years 1990–92 before beginning to rise again—slowly. In fact, it wasn't until 1998 that they passed the peak of that 1980s boom.[1] The millennial housing boom of 2000–05 was even bigger and faster than the 1980s boom, and history suggests that real estate prices will remain stagnant or even go down more than real estate agents would have us believe. It's another factor to consider.

Boom or bust, how can you know for sure that you are looking at the shelter issue rationally and uninfluenced by your money madness? I have a madness-free strategy you can use.

Rent vs. Buy: The Madness-Free Way to Get Your Home

The madness-free way to frame your home-shopping process is as a rent-versus-buy decision.

Chances are your first reaction to the idea is disbelief and/or disdain. The almost universally accepted assumption is that paying rent is just throwing money away. This assumption, like the one about the financial benefits of owning a home, needs to be challenged, for as with home ownership, notions about renting a home are heavily distorted by emotion.

For example, we tend to respond with a kind of emotional thumbs-up to the whole idea of home ownership. It carries with it a certain panache; it denotes soundness, wealth, earnestness, a fixed purpose.

By contrast, renting—especially if one has the means to own a home—is considered beneath one's dignity. It seems less fashionable, although the truth is that an awful lot of fashionable, wealthy people—people who could easily afford to own several homes—actually rent. They like the freedom from hassle and the idea that somebody else is responsible for maintenance and repairs.

But there's a sense of instability about renting. With leases typically of one or two years, renting seems to send a message that you're temporary; you're here for just a short while, not long enough to put down roots. It's true that tenants do not have total control over the length of their lease, and they are likely to make more moves in a lifetime than a homeowner. Whether this is bad or good, exhausting or exciting, is of course a subjective judgment.

In fact, the instability of renting can sometimes be a good thing. After all, you rent a car when you're on vacation. You rent a tuxedo when you're asked to be in a wedding. What you are paying for in these cases is the use of the item without any long-term responsibility; you don't have to find a place for either the car or the tux, don't have to keep either of them clean or tuned up, don't have to take them with you. In addition, renters have more flexibility to relocate for a job and reduce their fuel costs. No obligations can mean less stress—and less madness as well.

The very instability inherent in renting a house can sometimes offer a chance to take a madness-free, emotion-free look at where you want to live. I ran into my neighbor George some time ago, and he announced that he was moving the family from our town in the wine country to Silicon Valley to be nearer to his clients. They had sold their house not far from ours, had bought a house south of San Francisco, and were packing up to go. I wished him well.

A few months later, I was stunned to run into George back in the wine country. We greeted one another warmly. "How's Silicon Valley?" I asked.

"We're moving back," George replied. Although they liked both the new town and their new house, they missed the home and people they had left behind in our town. So at a cost of a $200,000 loss on the selling and buying of houses, George and the family were determined to become wine country residents again, only this time, they were going to rent first. In fact, what George most regretted about the whole costly roller-coaster event was that they hadn't rented in Silicon Valley for a year, trying it out, while perhaps leasing out the wine country house at the same time. They might have learned the lesson about where they wanted to live with far less disruption and certainly without the financial disaster. For George, the "instability" of renting was actually flexibility, which can be a good thing.

Or take the case of Abby, a retired teacher, recently widowed. Her plan was to sell the house she and her late husband had bought 35 years before—which she owned free and clear—buy a smaller, cheaper house in a less expensive town 45 minutes away, and invest the difference to supplement her income. As she figured it, if she forced herself to live frugally, she would continue to have all the standard benefits of home ownership—tax benefits, secure equity to fall back on, appreciation on the house, and a garden, although she would need to find a job that would pay at least $40,000 a year to make up the shortfall between even frugal expenses and the income from her investments.

But Abby was persuaded by a friend to challenge that assumption about home ownership and look hard at the numbers. And when she did, it quickly became clear that renting a house was a much better deal for her in every way. Investing all the proceeds of her house sale has provided her a much higher annual income than if she had bought another home. And now, instead of the $40,000 shortfall she would have as a homeowner, she faces an annual shortfall of $8,200, which she is easily making up in tutoring and music lessons. Plus, she gets to stay in her own neighborhood, among friends of a lifetime, and her landlord is thrilled that she wants to garden. Renting has become an unexpected symbol of freedom for Abby. (*Note:* The three scenarios Abby considered are detailed in the appendix.)

The madness-free strategy for home-shopping asks you to pit various assumptions against another: Does renting mean instability or flexibility? Is equity or income more important? When I put my clients through this exercise, I ask them to visit at least two and preferably three for-rent houses that are comparable to the house they're considering buying. I estimate it takes an afternoon at most to do so. Then I ask them to calculate the costs of buying versus renting. *All* the costs.

Rent-vs.-Buy Math Made Easy

The rent-vs.-buy calculation isn't as simple as the monthly mortgage payments if you've bought the house versus the monthly rent if you're on a lease. You need to include the initial costs and operating costs of both a potential purchase and an equivalent rental. Your goal is to tally the break-even point—that is, the number of years it takes for buying to be more financially advantageous than renting. That's something a lot of people fail to consider when they buy a house: How long will you have to live in it before you break even? Because statistics show that the average length of stay in a house is only about five years, that becomes a particularly important question to answer accurately.

Unfortunately, there's no formula for deciding how long you intend to live in a place. There's just your experience—your track record in your most recent homes, your personality, your level of restlessness, and some hard thinking to help you produce an answer—and the answer should probably be on the conservative side. You can ask friends who know you and your history how long they think you'll stay in this house. When clients ask my advice, I recommend that, for financial reasons at least, they should intend to stay in a house for 7 to 10 years.

Need a rule-of-thumb for the rent-versus-buy decision? *In financial terms only*, a general guideline is that it's a more viable financial proposition to buy when the purchase price is less than 20 times the annual cost of renting an equivalent home. And vice versa: Renting is more viable when the annual rental cost is less than 5 percent of the purchase price of an equivalent home. Let's take two equivalent houses in Philadelphia as an example; one is for sale at $250,000; the other rents for $1,100 a month—$13,200 a year. We see that 20 times the annual cost of renting is $264,000. And 5 percent of the purchase price is $12,500. So *in financial terms only*, it's marginally advantageous to buy rather than rent as a choice between these two. What's not part of this equation is the length of time you would live in either house and other housing-related costs.

So we come right back to the basic premise: You have to look at all the costs and do all the numbers carefully.

And Don't Forget the Cost of Money

One key number that potential homebuyers tend to forget or ignore is the annual opportunity cost of capital and the size of the interest portion of the mortgage payment. The opportunity cost of capital is what you're no longer earning in interest on the cash you took out of the bank or your portfolio to buy your house. Most homebuyers put down some money *and* take a mortgage, so they're both paying mortgage interest and not earning the interest on the cash they used for the down payment. Both must be figured into the annual cost of home ownership.

I've come up with a formula you can use to figure the annual cost of capital/amount of interest for a home you're thinking of buying. The formula calculates the percentage of the purchase price you'll have to add to the yearly cost of living in the house. (I've padded the formula a bit to take care of the transaction costs of buying and selling.) Here's how to figure your percentage:

- If you itemize your taxes and deduct mortgage interest, use the 30-year fixed mortgage rate, whatever that mortgage rate is at the time you're buying.
- If you don't itemize your taxes, multiply the 30-year fixed rate at the time you're buying by 1.25.

    Then multiply that percentage by the purchase price of the house, and that's your annual approximate cost of capital and/or of your mortgage interest payments.

For example, suppose you're considering a $500,000 house. With mortgage interest rates at about 6 percent as I write this, as an itemizing home buyer, you would pay $30,000 a year in cost of capital (6 percent x $500,000); as a nonitemizing home buyer, at 7.5 percent, you would pay $37,500 (7.5 percent x $500,000).

Following is a template that will help you keep track of the range of annual costs you need to consider as you compare buying that house you have your eye on with renting one of the two or three you looked at the other afternoon. Do the numbers. To ensure objectivity, look at your situation from the vantage of a third person; assume the perspective of a particular friend or just make up a person, then cast yourself in the role of that person's financial advisor. That way, you remove the emotion and free yourself from your money madness as you assess what it really costs to own and rent.

Annual Cost To . . .	
Buy	**Rent**
Cost of capital/amount of mortgage interest payments	Annual rent
Property taxes	
Homeowner's insurance	Renter's insurance
Maintenance and repairs	Maintenance and repairs
Long-term annual savings for large future repairs (for example, a new roof)	
Utilities, water	Utilities, water
Total	**Total**

For maintenance and repairs and long-term annual savings for large future repairs, I recommend estimating 1 percent and 0.75 percent of house value, respectively. Example: If a home costs $300,000, estimate $3,000 for annual maintenance and $2,225 for long-term annual savings.

Other Considerations?

You might also consider what you could gain if, instead of being forced to save via a mortgage, you rented a house and forced yourself to save through some sort of automatic deduction account. What would you earn if your automatic savings went into the Rainbow Portfolio invested in a Roth IRA account? Or what if you signed up for an automatic-deduction 401(k) and took advantage of your company's matching-contribution plan as well? What would be your gains? When I ran some numbers to answer these questions, I was surprised—even stunned—by the results. So were Donna and Jennifer, next-door neighbors in a new development—and longtime best friends.

Donna, a firm believer in the religion of home ownership, bought her $600,000 house in the development, lived in it for 10 years, and sold it for $1 million—the house having appreciated by even more than the national average over the 10-year period.[2] After taking advantage of the residential capital-gains-tax exclusion and paying off the mortgage and all transaction costs, Donna wound up with $450,000. Not bad.

During the same 10 years, Jennifer rented a house for around $2,100 a month, factoring in the rent increases over the years. But every month, she put aside $1,200, the difference between the ongoing costs of owning versus the ongoing costs of renting (see chart on p. 194), and invested it in the Rainbow Portfolio. She had started her Rainbow Portfolio with a lump sum investment that was the equivalent of what her down payment would have been had she bought the house instead of renting it: $120,000. With her Rainbow Portfolio having earned an average of 10 percent a year before taxes, at the end of the 10 years, when Jennifer too was ready to move, she had approximately $490,000 after taxes in the bank. Even better.

Again, I am in no way suggesting that the benefits of home ownership are a fallacy. I own my own home—for many of the reasons sold to us in the American dream: It's my family's castle where we can grow our own garden and redo our kitchen as we like. It offers a sense of stability and community that I think is particularly valuable for our young children; it's a pleasant and comfortable place to live, and we're pretty sure we'll stay in it long enough to break even, and then some. Wallet-wise, who knows? I'm not prepared to say the house is a can't-miss investment or that we wouldn't have more money and less bother if we rented.

Many people who do the numbers find that renting is not equivalent to throwing money down the drain after all—especially if you have the discipline to invest the cost differential that typically exists between buying and renting.

Moreover, just because you're renting doesn't mean you can't invest in real estate. The Rainbow Portfolio makes a significant commitment to real estate. And the fact is that many people who have made a fortune in real estate did so by renting their own homes and investing in commercial real estate.

The point is, you have to do the numbers. Then you're really ready to go shopping.

Spencer's Rules for Madness-Free Home Shopping
Here are my all-time top seven rules for house shopping. Abandon any one of them at your peril; you'll be inviting your money monster to take over again.

1. Look at two to three rentals comparable to the house or houses you're considering buying before you make a decision.
2. Ask yourself—and do a reality check with your friends—whether you will really stay in this house for at least 7 to 10 years, the average length of time it *usually* takes to break even financially on a house purchase relative to renting. Much less than that, and you limit the chance for the house to appreciate in value to any degree where buying becomes financially compelling.
3. Look at the most expensive house first. Just tell the real estate agent you want to start your "showings" at the top of your range. Experience and psychology have taught agents to do it the other way around, because it's been shown that the last thing in a series a person sees makes the biggest and most lasting impression. The expensive house, seen last, blows the moderate-priced houses out of the water. Done in reverse, the high-priced item is not so fresh in your mind, and the moderate-priced house can look just dandy—as well as enable you to keep some money in your pocket.
4. List three faults with the house you think you want

to buy, then calculate the cost of each negative. For example, if the picture window is cracked, what will it cost to replace it? If there's a super-highway beyond the backyard, what is the price tag for a soundproofing fence? At the moment, you have fallen in love, and as happens when you fall in love, your hormones are raging. Slow them down by forcing yourself to find and price these negatives.

5. Talk to the neighbors of the house you think you want to buy. If you were buying stock, you would do due diligence. Do it in this instance by asking the neighbors about the neighborhood, the house in question, the other neighbors. I'm shocked at how few people do this for the largest purchase they'll ever make.

6. See the house on a bad day. Come back when it's raining. Take a look at it at night. Drive over early one morning to check out the rush-hour traffic—for instance, how long does it take to back out of the driveway?

7. Do the rent-vs.-buy numbers. Evaluate *all* the costs for each. Remember my $70,000 first house that turned out to cost me $100,000—plus a lot of time and anxiety? That's why it's essential to calculate the cost of absolutely everything—schools, commute, heating, future repairs, yard maintenance—not just the sticker price. Only by weighing all factors can you ensure a level playing field for a financial decision. For help in doing so, go to www.curemoneymadness.com for the latest rent-vs.-buy calculator.

Then decide: Is owning this house a compelling financial proposition? If not, is it a compelling proposition in other ways? Are you sure you are aware of the difference between what is financially compelling and what is emotionally compelling?

What might be an alternative to owning the house—or at least, to owning it now?

There's a tendency when considering buying a home to think of it in a special way—as both a necessity and an investment, rather than as a purchase like any other—only much bigger and more expensive. By the same token, homeowners justify spending on the home as essential benefits that will add to the value of the investment—"We *need* those new windows!" But the dynamic of spending is actually the same as if we were buying a cashmere sweater or that high-def TV. Affordability needs to be the first question, and the answer must be based on a careful analysis of all the numbers. So answer all the questions above in a madness-free way and whatever you do, at least you won't be sabotaging your financial life to have a place you call home.

CHAPTER 9

Philanthropy and Money Madness

There's a funny irony at work when we talk about giving money away as charity or for philanthropy, and it's this: **When it comes to buying things, our money madness imbues us with the false notion that owning something is transformative; with it, we can change our world, change our lives. It isn't true. When it comes to philanthropy, our money madness tells us to expect nothing in return. The truth is that giving is transformative. When we give money, we really can change the world—and our lives—if we do it in a madness-free way. After all, we are the world.**

Yet the sad fact is that in our consumer society, giving charity has become one of those obligatory money transactions—as expected of us as home ownership or possession of the latest gadget. What do I mean by *obligatory?* You know the kind of thing: After being solicited earnestly by that nice-sounding young woman over the phone, you agree to send a donation. Or because everyone else at work is giving to this particular charity, you figure you'd better write a check as well. Or it's the building fund drive for your church; how can you possibly not give? Such transactions prompt as much stress as any other money chore—maybe more—and we sometimes do them just as thoughtlessly, driven, as always, by the emotions of our personal money monster.

My childhood money message when it came to charity was that the big charitable organizations were suspect. They were not to be trusted. After all, you couldn't see into them, so how could you know for sure what they were doing with the money they were given? Naturally, this attitude was driven by my core childhood money message that money is security, you can never have enough of it, and you must never speak about it. Giving money to these big nameless organizations flew in the face of all of that: Money went out, but you had no firm control over what it did, and at the same time, the act of giving was a public signal that you had enough to donate.

This is not to say there was no model of charity in our family. On the contrary, my father was instinctively generous with aid when and where it was needed, almost always spontaneously. But, in keeping with everything else about money in our house, I observed these gifts being given, but we never discussed them.

By the time I was working and in a position to donate some money and time of my own, charitable giving had become the very opposite of what I learned at home. It was now another item on the consumer's checklist; it was not only important to give, it was politically correct and socially advantageous to talk about it, to be seen to give. Your tote bag proclaimed you a donor to the public television station. Your umbrella identified you as a contributor to a medical cure. You announced your charitable giving on your T-shirt or baseball cap or with the coffee mug you brought into the office—the equivalent of the brightly colored plastic bracelets people today wear on their wrists; by your "premiums" you were known—as was the level of your giving.

Those visible tokens of philanthropy to some extent shamed people like me into giving, but they also showed that giving was now another expense expected of us, part and parcel of being a consumer in the consumer society. I gave money to the causes my friends and clients and acquaintances gave to because they did; and sometimes I gave money because I saw a telethon that moved me or because a well-written letter arrived in the mail urging me to donate money to what sounded like a worthy cause. It was all of a piece with all the rest of the mindless spending I did in the course of the day and had little to do with true generosity.

And it was all money madness. Just as I responded to the latest investment tip, I was responding to the latest charity solicitation. Just as I followed where the active investors put their money, I followed where my colleagues and friends gave their money, giving *reactively*—like attending the "Lung Disease Dinner" because a client was chairman of the committee. I have no idea how much I gave, or what percentage of my income it represented. It was all done mindlessly. If anyone had asked me what I got out of my charitable giving, I suppose I would have answered: the tax deduction. It seemed to me there had to be a better way to give.

Philinvesting

One alternative is well suited to people who are uncomfortable with standard charitable giving or want to supplement their giving. It is a way to turn your investing habit into philanthropy. I call it "philinvesting." And while it does not entail literally giving money away, it is philanthropy just the same. By combining investing with philanthropy, philinvesting expands our definition of both.

Take the example of a client of mine who makes $1 million a year and has routinely made annual charitable donations totaling a mere $100. The reason for such lack of generosity? Simple. This is a man who sees charitable giving as a "handout"—something with which he is constitutionally—perhaps congenitally—uncomfortable. So apart from a small gift to his son's school, mostly so the boy won't be embarrassed, he simply has no interest in traditional philanthropic giving.

But this year, he is investing a sizable amount of money in microfinance institutions in India and Africa. Whether he knows it or not, he is being philanthropic—but without giving money away. He's also acting in complete accord with his personal values, which applaud even the smallest-scale capitalism. The investment he is making is riskier than most of the other investments in his portfolio, but he is excited about lending small amounts of money to help the world's poorest people rise out of poverty. Like a lot of people, he likes the corporate for-profit model of the fund in which he has invested—its accountability, fiscal discipline, and strong management processes; and he is looking forward to returns, in time, that he hopes may yield as much as 15 percent on his investment—which he might then reinvest in another philinvestment, building even more social capital.

It's the perfect definition of philinvesting. Instead of donating money, you invest it—but in a way that you believe benefits humankind or brings the kinds of change you want to see—and you get a financial return for doing so, plus the personal satisfaction that can come from helping transform the world for the better.

Worried about global warming? Why not invest in renewable energy funds or in companies developing products or processes aimed at reducing the impact of fossil fuels? If the investment does well, both you as the investor and the world at large will benefit. If the investment fails, all you lose is the money you would have given to charity anyway.

The range of options for philinvesting—making money and making a difference at the same time—is as wide as your philanthropic interests, but for some ideas, check out my website at www.cure moneymadness.com.

Madness-Free Giving: Making an Investment, Getting a Return

Philinvesting has something to teach those who give to charity as well, for in my view, it makes sense to look on charitable giving as an investment—an opportunity that can yield a return. To test this assertion, ask yourself how much of your charitable giving goes to charities that don't solicit you.

Chances are the answer is close to zero. We tend to be passive givers. We wait for the charity to come to us: the solicitation letter, the person-to-person phone call, the telethon with exhausted celebrities showing off the poster child with the cajoling smile.

Strategic thinking is as foreign to our charitable giving as is expecting a return. The former sounds like what you do when you're investing money, not giving it away. The latter sounds selfish.

That's exactly how charitable giving should be approached, however—like an investment opportunity from which you selfishly expect a return. There's really only one question to ask when you give money to a charity: What will change as a result of my donation? As with investing, you are putting your money to work; you should expect in return that the world will be a better place as a result. Our consumer society tells us to feel shame for *not* giving money away with abandon; on the contrary, we should feel shame for giving it away with as much abandon as we do, without insisting on a way to measure the results we produce for the world.

The selfishness works on several levels. If we give money to help cure avian flu in Asia, for example, we get a return on two counts. First, fewer people will die of avian flu—that is a benefit all its own, and we can feel good for bringing life-saving help to individuals thousands of miles away. Second, we can say that making inroads against a potential pandemic literally lessens the chances we ourselves will become infected—and we can certainly feel safer as a result. Both results are important, both the sense of doing good in the world and the sense of keeping illness at bay, even if both may be seen as self-serving.

Once we accept the idea of investment and return on investment—once we accept our own selfishness—then we can focus on which organization most effectively and efficiently buys us the world transformation we want for our money.

The Madness-Free Charitable Giving Strategy

First of all, decide how much money you are prepared to give away each year. Think in percentages, not dollar figures, so that you will always be giving appropriately whether your income goes up or down. My wife and I devote either 10 percent of our annual after-tax income or 1 percent of our net worth to charitable giving, whichever is greater; either, however, is a pretty good standard. If you're wary of giving, or if you're uncomfortable with numbers, start small—with 1 percent of your cash flow or 0.1 percent of your net worth. Over time, increase the percentage of your giving until you start getting diminishing returns—that is, until the expanded giving is no longer expanding your satisfaction and sense of well-being. My bet—and I've seen this in myself as well as in my clients—is that you will go a very long way before reaching that point of diminishing returns, if ever.

Once you have determined the portion of your income or net worth you'll be giving, you need to identify the categories or change you want to create in the world—maybe the environment, or fighting a particular disease, or education. In other words, you need to consider your values and determine what you care about when you think about changing the world. Here are two good ways to do this.

First, for the next week, as you read the morning paper, circle three things you want more of in the world and three things you want less of. That will help tell you what you want your money to advance and/or what you want it to retard.

Second, at the same time, talk to friends. Charitable giving is another one of those money secrets we tend not to discuss. Maybe, after working through the awareness cure for your money madness, you now know more about your friends' money values and where they invest, but do you know to whom they give their money? **Finding out may give you some ideas; it will also tell more about your friends' values and may prompt you to understand your own.**

Once you've identified these categories of change, allot percentages to each. Maybe you decide that you want to commit 30 percent of your giving to improving the environment, 20 percent to battling cancer, and the rest to education projects you're not yet sure about. In fact, I recommend saving 20 percent for unplanned, discretionary gifts—spontaneous giving you can do throughout the year.

Only now do you start looking for the organizations to give to. And only when you've found them will you decide how to apportion your giving—whether you'll give the total allotment for a category to one organization or split it among several.

It's in exploring the individual organizations that you will keep an eye out for the efficiencies and levels of effectiveness my father was always worried about. Start by asking boldly how the organization measures its performance and what results it has produced over time. But don't stop there. Today, with charitable organizations closely regulated and with public disclosure universally required, the information you need on any single organization is typically no farther away than the Internet. Try www.charitynavigator.org, the Better Business Bureau's wise giving site (www.give.org), and/or the attorney general's office of the state in which the organization is domiciled.

You want to be sure the charity does what it says it does, does it reasonably well, and is fiscally sound. One way to check on fiscal soundness is to look at the organization's Form 990 (its required annual IRS form), and you can find these on the Web at GuideStar (www.guidestar.org). There is no dearth of information available for assuring yourself of the worth of just about any charitable organization. And as always, check with www.curemoneymadness.com for more references and updating of existing references.

Find at least three charities that match your values and answer your interest in changing the world. Over the next three months, call one a month. Tell them you want to contribute, unsolicited, to their work. Tell them you will give money or an in-kind donation, but that you want to get involved, you want to see their offices, meet the people the charity is helping, watch them advance their work. Dedicate these three months to deciding which organizations you'd like to put at the top of your list.

Here's how my wife and I execute our charitable giving strategy. We split our total giving into two halves. We donate one half jointly, and we each reserve 50 percent of the other half to do separately. The separate giving decreases our individual money madnesses by endowing each of us with a sense of freedom and spontaneity, while the joint giving increases our financial intimacy. In addition, a portion of our giving is dedicated to charities our children decide on; we match the funds they donate out of their allowance.

In all, we contribute to some 20 different organizations, in varying proportions, but most of our joint giving is organized around the broad categories that are our focus: early childhood education, sustainable farming, and conflict resolution. Those themes drive our giving for the year. It means that if a friend asks us to save the whales, we must say no—at least for this year. I love whales, and I want them to be saved, but in giving, once you determine which values you'll advance, it makes sense to buy and hold. Do what the great philanthropists have always done, from Andrew Carnegie to Bill Gates: Find your focus, strategize for it, and stick to it. It's the opposite of what we do with investing, where diversification is the goal. With philanthropy, my clients and I find that we make a bigger impact by concentrating on fewer organizations. It's a good way to change the world.

One more point: Money isn't the only gift you can give an organization. If time is money, then spending time enhances both the value you're donating and the satisfaction you'll get in return. Giving money is a spectator sport; giving time, in addition to money or instead of money, means being part of the charity's results in the world, not just receiving a progress report on those results.

The Charity Opportunity: Giving to Get

Giving to a charity or cause without waiting to be contacted is an exceptionally good way to break through your money madness. In fact, all charitable giving, done with eyes open, thoughtfully, and strategically, connects you with the world in ways you cannot imagine. Thanks to the Internet, you can now laser-target your giving—whatever the amount—to not just your particular interest, but to a specific project that addresses that interest, and even to a specific person directing the project. For example, there's an education charity website—www.donorschoose.org—that lets you target a particular location, a particular school, even a specific classroom need, then send money directly to the teacher of that class. This facilitates a level of intimacy between the individual and his or her philanthropic purpose that has simply not been possible heretofore. And how gratifying it is to see, almost literally, the specific benefit your act of charity is achieving. (Check my website, www.curemoneymadness.com, for more such sites.)

I know precisely how it feels to see that specific benefit. I had given money for years with no return on my "investment," no real idea where the money was going, and no interest in the effectiveness of my giving. It was a rote exercise; the money monster said do it, and I wrote the check. There was nothing of me in the transaction whatsoever.

Then some years ago, I heard about an organization that promotes conflict resolution in schools by empowering students to dissolve conflict on their own, without relying on adults. The opportunity to invest in young people as self-reliant change agents for peace was very inspiring to me, and when I was given the opportunity to sponsor a workshop at our local school, I was eager to do so. This time, when I wrote out a check, I got back for it a specific program in my hometown. And when I saw the program at work—when I watched the kids resolving conflicts peacefully—something inside me changed substantively.

I gave away money to help make this happen, I thought to myself, and all my childhood fears about never being able to have enough money suddenly dissolved. The money monster withdrew, taking my money madness with him. Money had flowed away from me, and I wasn't hysterical about it. On the contrary. What I had just bought was a feeling of generosity that seemed to change my cellular structure. *Maybe money isn't survival,* I thought. *After all, I just gave it away and didn't die from it. In fact, strangely enough, I feel wealthier!* Hey, I realized, *I do have enough.*

CHAPTER 10

Enough—Finding Your Sufficiency

In 1995, I took a trip to New Mexico and went on a trek through the desert. It was like a scene from the movie *City Slickers:* New York boy confronts utter barrenness and is totally out of his element. The environment consisted of rocks, dry earth, and endless sky. I was prepared with only the food and water in my pack and the clothes I was wearing. There were no people to talk to, few plants to break the monotony of the desert landscape. There was no more and no less, no future and no past. Just the present.

All I did in this environment—and I had to do it all—was walk, breathe, listen to lizards scurry out from under rocks, keep my eye on the trail, and stop now and again to drink, look at the vista, and consider where I was. As I did so, a funny thing happened to my money monster. He evaporated. He simply seemed to dry up in the vastness of the Southwestern desert. There, all that counted was the ground under my feet and my strength to move across it. In the face of these realities, there was suddenly no desire for more money, no fantasy about hitting the jackpot on a stock tip, no calculations about how to beat the market so I could get a bigger house or faster car. House, car, salary, retirement portfolio became accessories to the central wealth I possessed: a canteen of water, legs moving, brain thinking, heart beating, eyes seeing, ears alert to every sound.

They say the desert light gives a kind of clarity. I'll vouch for it, because suddenly I saw the real sufficiency of all that I possessed—the ability to earn money, yes, but alongside it my health, my friends, my family, my colleagues at work, my untapped skills and creativity, my power to laugh, speak, listen, smell, touch, taste, feel, think, contribute to the world, and move myself along the desert trail.

That there was value in all of these things was indisputable. They are, as all will agree, among the things that make life worth living, and surely they are worth as much, in terms of quality of life, as the value of my bank and brokerage accounts.

The revelation in the desert, however, was not only the intrinsic value of all these attributes but their financial worth. The epiphany was that these were possessions as real as my house and car. They were assets to be prized as highly as stocks in a portfolio.

That surprised me. And it occurred to me, as I trudged along the dusty trail under a piercing sun, that there were three ways I could measure these possessions and assets monetarily.

First, if any one of them were taken away, I would pay to get it back. We're always reluctant to put a price on a body part or speak in terms of material value about people we love, because these "possessions" are priceless beyond calculation. Yet there in the desert, I began to consider what I would pay to have strong legs that could walk for a full day—should those legs collapse out from under me. The answer was obvious: I would pay anything and everything. I would pay all I have. Similarly, I could measure the worth of each of my newly defined assets by estimating just how much I would pay to retrieve each if they were taken away—or to obtain them, if I lacked them to begin with.

Second, the value of each of these possessions, when assessed relative to the standard material possessions listed on a net worth statement, was in fact greater than the material possession. For example, what economic value would I place on my health relative to the economic value of my house? In other words, would I rather be a sick billionaire or a healthy homeless person? The latter, for sure.

Third, each of these possessions affected my ability to make more money in the marketplace. Common wisdom would have it that a sense of humor, for example, while a wonderful thing to possess, has no material value. "It won't pay the rent," people tell you.

What I understood in the desert, however, was that a sense of humor did in fact have material value. It would make me better at my job—any job: a better teacher, salesperson, lawyer, contractor. I understood that work colleagues constituted a support system that would make me a better financial advisor. My senses of touch, taste, smell, sight, and hearing made me more attuned to the marketplace, my clients, and my employees. The difference each of these made to my marketplace value could be measured positively (that is, harmonious family relations helped me be a contented, confident CEO making sound decisions) or negatively (that is, an argument with my wife could sour my mood and depress my ability to inspire employees and seize the financial moment). Therefore, all of those measures could and should be assets or liabilities to my total net worth, for they had calculable material impact on my ability to earn and on my market value.

Didn't that then mean that my total net worth—my actual net worth—really went beyond what I could measure in stocks, bonds, real estate, and cash on hand? And if that were the case, didn't that mean that my actual net worth was really quite a bit more considerable than I had once estimated it?

Yes, it meant exactly that.

You Are More Than Your Net Worth

I've seen the truth of my revelation in the desert time and again. I look at the Randolphs, the contractors who lost their house and just about every penny they had and finally declared bankruptcy. Are they poor because they have no money? I can't see them as such. They have each other, wonderful children, an abundance of skills. They're intelligent about most things—except perhaps about resolving their money madness—and they bring to their situation a shared cheerfulness of outlook that is compelling. They are ready to turn their lives around, they believe they have the tools to do it, and they are confident they will do it.

Count it up. Aren't those possessions as rich a supply of resources as a pile of dollars in the bank? Think of the squirrel whose supply of nuts for the winter has been swiped by a fox or swooped up by a falcon. He's down but by no means out; he still possesses all the speed, maneuverability, and adaptability—not to mention an all-purpose tail—that got him his hoard of food in the first place; he can do it again. Same with the Randolphs. Their storehouse of value, although devoid of nuts—read: *cash*—for the moment, is still filled with other resources: intelligence, will, strength, sense of humor. They're not poor at all.

I want to be very clear about this. I am not talking about the abstract, spiritual value of these resources, although I take that value seriously as well. Rather, I mean the economic market value of the resources. Actual net worth, in my view, consists of more than the assets and liabilities on the net worth statement you drew up in Chapter 5. To those assets and liabilities, you really need to add two things: the value of your future lifetime income *and* the very material worth of the resources that are making those earnings possible.

To calculate the former, take your current annual compensation or marketplace value, and multiply it by the number of years you estimate will constitute your future work life, based on your health. If your after-tax earnings come to $70,000 a year and grow by inflation each year, and if you expect you'll work another 25 years, then the present value of your future earnings is just 25 times $70,000 or $1.75 million. That's not chump change; it's substantive.

Calculating the latter—the market value of the resources you possess that are enabling you to gain those earnings—is a bit different. I'm not sure you can give a precise dollar value to your health and fitness, to the friends who enrich your life, to your untapped skills and creativity, and to the sense of humor that keeps you balanced, but I am absolutely certain that these attributes are assets—worth more than zero—that should be added up as part of your actual net worth.

Want to give it a try? Where your health is concerned, how much money would make it worth your while to risk a chronic illness, a disability, or a shortened life span? What friendships would you give up to gain money? As for a sense of humor, don't think it has no marketplace power. I have known middle manager after middle manager who never rose in the hierarchy, not because they didn't have the intelligence and will and motivation, but simply because at a certain point, they reached the limit of their ability to see beyond a narrow context as they interacted with others. It's precisely that kind of perspective that a sense of humor provides, and it's why it's one of the most valuable, marketable, financially important assets you can have—something well worth accounting for when you ask yourself the question, How much is enough?

So add these five items to the net worth statement you prepared in Chapter 5:

- Future lifetime income.
- Friends and family.
- Untapped skills and creativity.
- Health.
- Sense of humor/perspective.

And now add up your Actual Net Worth.

Your Actual Net Worth	
Assets	**Value**
Liquid assets	
Bank accounts	
CDs	
Money markets	
Total liquid assets	
Investment assets	
Brokerage accounts	
Mutual funds	
Business assets	
Total investment assets	
Retirement assets	
IRAs	
Employer-sponsored retirement plan	
Total retirement assets	

Assets	Value
Real estate assets	
Primary residence	
Second or vacation home	
Rental properties	
Total real estate assets	
Human assets	
Future lifetime income	
Friends and family	
Untapped skills and creativity	
Health	
Sense of humor/perspective	
Total human assets	
Total assets	
Liabilities	
Personal loans	
Credit cards	
Mortgage(s)/home equity loans	
Business loans	
Student loans	
Other	
Total liabilities	
ACTUAL NET WORTH (total assets — total liabilities)	

Seeing your Actual Net Worth—the economic value of *all* your assets—can shatter your fixed ideas about money, whether you're rich or poor by traditional standards of net worth. It's a reminder that you yourself, not a banker or broker, are the person responsible for defining your worth. That's why the Actual Net Worth statement can change your sense of yourself, your relations with others, even your life. One workshop participant who came into the workshop thinking he had a net worth of $4,132—thanks to having taken on too much debt—left thinking he had an Actual Net Worth of more than $4 million. He said the realization shifted just about everything in his life. Over the next several months, he stopped seeing himself as a lackluster breadwinner and lackluster husband, went after a new job and got it, and stopped fearing rich people because he now saw himself as rich as well.

Another participant saw that the $10 million she had in the bank paled by comparison to her Actual Net Worth. It has made her far less fearful about the money in the bank, which she now invests and donates with much greater confidence and which she is using to make a real difference in the world.

So look at both statements, the traditional net worth statement and your Actual Net Worth statement. Which looks more true to you? Which assessment is more real?

Find Your Number

"What's your number?"

That's what the young, hotshot, Armani-suited equities and currency traders used to ask one another back in Wall Street's boom-boom days. The answer was the dollar figure each trader thought would be enough to quit work altogether and still luxuriate in the extravagant lifestyle they believed they had earned. Once he hit his number, he'd be gone—zooming off to his Caribbean hideaway for some marlin fishing. And she'd be jetting around the world—first class—with time in luxury hotels to write her long-dreamed-of novel. No sweat.

Most money books tell you how to keep on adding to your net

worth so you can feed these fantasies; this book alerts you to the reality that there's no sufficiency when you achieve a particular number, because your money monster will remind you that you can always add one more dollar to your bank account, a new stock to your portfolio, another shed to your real estate holdings. This book tells you that sufficiency is now; if you believe it's coming to you in the future, you'll always believe it—and sufficiency will never come. It's endless because there's no way to define "enough" and thus no way to satisfy the definition. That's why the boom-boom boys and girls always upped their number once they met it; it's a moving target.

Only if you define sufficiency as value in the here-and-now can you ever achieve it. To see what I mean, try what I call the Five-and-Five Exercise, or the Last Five and the Top Five.

Name the five biggest purchases you made over the last five years—lawn-mowing tractor, digital camera, pearl necklace, exercise equipment, silk dress. How often and how much do you still use these items—and do they mean as much now as they seemed to just before you bought them?

Now name the five things you really value out of all the things you have—both material and nonmaterial possessions. Assume that you have to give away everything except these five. What are they—the top five things you will hold on to no matter what? For me, for example, my top five are my health, my intelligence, my circle of friends and family, my sense of humor, and my service to the world.

Your top five are indubitably all that you need, and surely a person who has all that he or she needs is rich. That's you. If you can imagine taking away from yourself everything except these five, you have tamed your money monster; if you can see the richness the five represent, you can find your sufficiency.

The Rewards of Sufficiency

Enormous energy is unleashed when we throw off the anxieties of money madness and find our sufficiency. *This is enough*, you say to yourself; life is clarified, and stress and striving finally dissolve. It amounts to nothing less than a liberation. School is out, summer is here, the pressure is off.

A single mother employed as an administrative assistant in the small branch office of a large accounting firm, Eleanor grew up with the childhood money message that "things will work out." The result was that she simply took no responsibility for money, distancing herself from everything that had anything to do with the subject. Yes, she held a job, and yes, she and her family lived simply enough. But the fact was that her job brought very little to the family coffers, and that it in no way used Eleanor's talents or realized her potential.

In many ways, that was fine with Eleanor. Work that didn't involve her too significantly, demand too much of her, or hold her too accountable to any sort of standard accorded nicely with the way she distanced herself from money. After all, if things would work out, if the money would take care of itself somehow, then so would the job; it just didn't pay to step forward and take charge of either.

Until the stress of being unable to keep up with her bills got to her and the credit card debt engulfed her. That's when Eleanor came to my workshop on curing money madness. Hearing others talk about their money madness helped Eleanor see her own madness—and how her money behavior might influence her children. Where many in the workshop that weekend focused too much on money, Eleanor saw that her madness was to pretend it wasn't there. Where others futilely sought happiness in money, she saw that she already felt happiness apart from money and would just as soon have nothing to do with money at all. What Eleanor shared with other participants, however, was fear where money was concerned—in Eleanor's case, a fear of taking responsibility for money, a fear even of looking at money objectively.

What she gained from examining her Actual Net Worth in that weekend workshop was the courage to do a reality check. "What do I need?" Eleanor asked herself. "In dollar terms, how much money do I need if I am going to contribute in a responsible way to my family's well-being?" She sat down and looked at the numbers. They told her, in black and white, that she was 20 percent short on meeting the expenses she ought to be paying. The numbers also showed her exactly

CHAPTER 11

Make It Happen

One day last year, as Janine and I were preparing dinner in the kitchen, I opened the pantry door looking for something, and my eyes fell on a jar of capers. Now, I know that capers are a condiment considered a delicacy by many, but our family never eats them, so their appearance in our pantry was startling, out of place.

"What's this jar of capers doing here?" I asked my wife. "We don't eat them."

"No," she replied, "but we often have guests who like them in their salad."

The capers seemed to glare at me, and suddenly, I could feel the old terror wash over me. *It's throwing money away!* I thought to myself. *These capers we don't eat cost $4.89! It may not seem like much, but how many times can we squander even $4.89 before we're out on the streets?* I felt tension rise within me, could sense anger taking over, and I heard myself raise my voice to my wife. "We're spending money on things we don't like because future guests may want them some day? That is wasteful! Unacceptable!"

Janine looked up from the salad bowl and regarded me as if I were either crazy or a jerk.

In fact, I was both. My money madness was back.

It's the warning I gave you at the very start of this book: *Our childhood money messages keep playing for life.* They keep rousing that money monster that lurks under the bed, and the money monster keeps urging us to go and do some foolish thing or act in some irrational and potentially destructive way.

Get used to it: It will continue to happen. You can only tame the monster; you can never really be rid of him. Saboteurs lurk everywhere, so here are some tips to help you keep them at bay.

Tip 1
Keep Your Intentions Reasonable

Every January, health club membership soars. Sated after the excesses of the holidays, we vow to get back in shape—fast. Partied out, overfed, and sluggish, we commit ourselves to a full hour at the health club every day.

It's a setup for failure—too much too soon—and we're soon slashing the hour to a half hour and the every-day commitment to every other day—at best. And after a while, rather than confront our failed commitment, we just forget about the gym altogether.

The same thing happens with curing money madness. If we try for too much too soon, we quickly find ourselves making excuses for our noncompliance, then just forgetting the whole thing. So ease into it. Set a reasonable intention that will challenge you but not defeat you. Start small, and appreciate each gain.

Do you typically check the markets once an hour? Start by committing to once a day, not by vowing you'll only look once a month. Are you a shopaholic? Don't promise yourself you'll never again set foot in a mall; make a promise you can keep—like going to the mall once a week on Wednesday from noon to 2:00 P.M. In other words, make a *reasonable* plan, one with a sustainable hurdle that stirs your intention and is within your capabilities. And stick to it. The mantra I use to my employees is: *Small intentions lead to small successes, which create success overall. Large intentions too often lead to struggle and disappointment, which create failure overall.*

Tip 2
Keep a Money Diary

The reason behind recommending that dieters keep a food diary is that the process of logging every single thing you eat can actually help you control the eating. If you're writing it down, you're forced to be mindful about your eating—and mind can beat emotion.

That's the idea behind keeping a money diary. It might look something like the following chart:

Date/Time	Transaction/ Money Interaction	Emotion Felt	Connection to Childhood Money Message

But the truth is, your money diary doesn't have to follow any format whatsoever. Simply spending 10 minutes a day writing about your money transactions, your money fears, your money desires, and your money intentions can achieve the same purpose as a prescripted layout.

Tip 3
The Power of Two—Or More

One of the best ways to ensure that you stay on the road to the cure for money madness is to do it with others. Find a mutual money mentor—someone who can be an objective sounding board to keep you to your intentions, and whom you can keep on track too. Or what about starting a Cure Money Madness conversation in your church group, your men's group, your Rotary Club meeting—anywhere you and your peers can offer one another assistance, information, encouragement, and that all-important element of the cure—objective feedback. (Check out my website, www.curemoneymadness.com, for more information on how to do it.)

Tip 4
Set Your Personal Ground Rules

If you know there's something you can't resist, try to get it out of the way. In my case, it was mail-order catalogs. I couldn't say no, which is why our downstairs closet is clogged with clock radios I haven't

APPENDIX

Abby's Dilemma

Abby is a teacher, recently retired from the school system, and recently widowed. Naturally, she is looking hard at her assets and her future as she approaches some key decisions about money and lifestyle.

She has figured out that she needs about $50,000 a year to live—to maintain her house, her car, and herself, and to pay taxes, insurance, utilities, and the normal expenses of living. To achieve this $50,000, she has a schoolteacher's pension of $12,000 a year plus her income from giving piano lessons. Recently, a number of her students have stopped taking lessons, and Abby is aware that piano teaching is not a growth business and that she is living well beyond her means.

Her house, which she and her late husband bought 35 years ago for $125,000—and which she owns free and clear—is today worth $650,000. To make ends meet, Abby has therefore decided to sell her house, buy another for $400,000 in a less expensive town 45 minutes away, and invest the $250,000 difference to supplement her income.

Why would she give up the comforts and familiarity of a community where she has lived for more than three decades? Abby offers the standard answer: She would do so to have the benefits of owning her own home. What are those benefits? Again, Abby answers by rote: tax benefits, secure equity to fall back on that she can't touch unless she absolutely needs it, and appreciation on the house—not to mention being able to live without fear of a landlord not renewing a lease, being able to decorate and garden with abandon, and enjoying the pride of ownership. It is the standard money madness message that Abby has known since the age of four.

And then she takes a look at the numbers:

Scenario One: Abby Stays Put

Pension income	$12,000
Total income	$12,000*
Total expenses	$50,000
The shortfall Abby has to earn to pull even	$38,000

Note: Of course her $650,000 house will probably appreciate by about 4.2 percent per year on average. But she can't spend the income from the appreciation until she sells the house.

Scenario Two: Abby Sells Her House and Buys Another

Pension income	$12,000
Proceeds from house transactions after closing costs	$204,500
Income from portfolio created with proceeds of the house sale	$12,270*
Total Income	$24,270
Expenses and taxes	$46,300†
The shortfall Abby has to earn to pull even	$22,030

Here Abby's balanced Rainbow Portfolio grows at 11 percent per year. Take away 1.65 percent for taxes, and Abby is earning 9.35 percent per year. She withdraws 6 percent ($12,270) and nets 3.35 percent per year to allow for future inflation-adjusted withdrawals.

†*Abby's expenses are down because in this scenario, she has moved to a house with lower maintenance and utility costs, even though she is paying higher property taxes.*

Scenario Three: Abby Sells Her House and Rents

Pension income	$12,000
Proceeds from house transactions after closing costs	$610,000
Income from portfolio created with proceeds of the house sale	$36,000*
Total income	$48,600
Annual rent expense	$22,800
Other expenses and taxes	$34,000
Total expenses	$56,800
The shortfall Abby has to earn to pull even	$8,200

Here Abby's balanced Rainbow Portfolio grows at 11 percent per year. Take away 1.65 percent in taxes, and she's getting 9.35 percent per year. She withdraws 6 percent ($36,600) and she's netting 3.35 percent per year to allow for future inflation-adjusted withdrawals or for growth on the Rainbow Portfolio to offset the house appreciation she's now giving up.

It's fair to say that looking at the numbers shifted Abby's emotions. Today, at age 58, she loves the freedom of knowing that she has to earn only $8,200 a year to make ends meet—as opposed to $22,000 or $38,000.* She now rents a pleasant house two blocks away from her former home. Much of the living room is consumed by the concert grand piano, on which she continues to give piano lessons, which, along with tutoring, earn her enough to pull even. She asked for and got a five-year lease on the house and is putting in a garden. She loves knowing that if something goes wrong with the house, it's someone else's responsibility to fix it.

*The $22,800 in annual rent equals $1,900 in monthly rent. Even if her rent were $2,400 per month, her annual shortfall would only increase from $8,200 to $14,200 per year. Renting is still her best option.

NOTES

Chapter I

1. Daphne Merkin, "Our Money, Our Selves," *New Yorker*, April 26 and May 3, 1999, pp. 88–104.

Chapter 6

1. Several studies have confirmed it. See "The Percent of Large U.S. Stock Funds That Underperformed the S&P," by Burton Malkiel, Princeton economics professor and a director at Vanguard.
2. Charles D. Ellis, *Winning the Loser's Game* (McGraw-Hill, 2002).
3. Jeff Brown, "Beating Index Funds Takes Rare Luck or Genius," *Philadelphia Inquirer*, October 12, 2004.
4. On September 18, 2006, the law firm of Schlichter, Bogard & Denton filed the first wave of lawsuits regarding 401(k) plan fees.

Chapter 8

1. David Leonhardt, "A Word of Advice During a Housing Slump: Rent," *New York Times*, April 11, 2007.
2. Based on figures from the Office of Federal Housing Enterprise Oversight.

ABOUT THE AUTHOR

SPENCER SHERMAN, MBA, has been named one of *Worth* magazine's top wealth advisors every year since 2005. He is the founder and CEO of Abacus Wealth Partners LLC. He leads workshops on curing money madness with bestselling author Byron Katie and with relationship expert Anne Watts. He lives in northern California with his wife and two children. His Web site is www.curemoneymadness.com.

THE RAINBOW PORTFOLIO

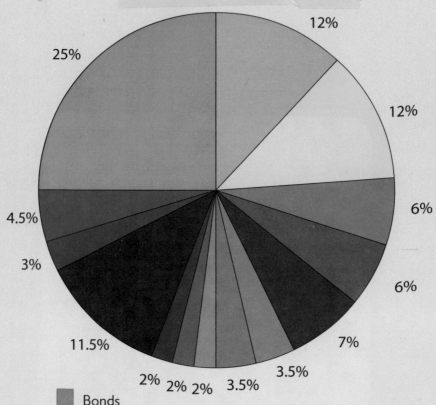

- Bonds
- U.S. large
- U.S. large value
- U.S. small
- U.S. small value
- International large value
- International small
- International small value
- Emerging markets large
- Emerging markets small
- Emerging markets value
- U.S. real estate
- International real estate
- Commodities